TortoiseSVN 1.7
Beginner's Guide

Perform version control in the easiest way with the best SVN client – TortoiseSVN

Lesley Harrison

PUBLISHING

BIRMINGHAM - MUMBAI

TortoiseSVN 1.7
Beginner's Guide

First published: January 2011

Production Reference: 1311210

Published by Packt Publishing Ltd.
32 Lincoln Road
Olton
Birmingham, B27 6PA, UK.

ISBN 978-1-849513-44-9

www.packtpub.com

Cover Image by Asher Wishkerman (a.wishkerman@mpic.de)

Credits

Author
Lesley Harrison

Reviewers
Robert Dudus

Stefan Küng

Eric Poole

Acquisition Editor
Tarun Singh

Development Editor
Tarun Singh

Technical Editors
Gauri Iyer

Prashant Macha

Indexer
Hemangini Bari

Editorial Team Leader
Mithun Sehgal

Project Team Leader
Ashwin Shetty

Project Coordinator
Michelle Quadros

Proofreader
Samantha Lyon

Graphics
Nilesh Mohite

Production Coordinator
Adline Swetha Jesuthas

Cover Work
Adline Swetha Jesuthas

About the Author

Lesley Harrison has more than ten years experience working in the world of IT. She has served as a web developer for the local government, a systems administrator for a multinational IT outsourcing company, and a database administrator for a British utility company. Today, Lesley runs her own video gaming site, `Myth-Games.com`, and works as a freelance web developer.

In her spare time Lesley volunteers within several Open Source projects. Away from the computer she recently found a love for Seiken Ryu Karate, and has reached the rank of 4th Kyu.

I would like to thank my husband, Mark, for his endless patience, and the wonderful gesture of building a spare machine to use as a server for testing.

I would also like to thank Stefan Küng (TortoiseSVN) and Robert Dudus, for their eagle-eyed technical reviewing, which shaped this book into what you see today.

About the Reviewers

Robert Dudus has been a developer for over 5 years. During this time, he has designed and developed applications in widely varying areas such as computer video games, bioinformatics, web design, property searches, and loans.

He has first-hand developer experience with C++, Java, C#, and technologies around them. He considers himself a pragmatic programmer. He doesn't stand on formality and he's willing to look at alternate or unorthodox solutions to a problem if that's what it takes.

Robert is currently employed by Inform Link Limited in London, UK, as a software developer/analyst in the centralized development group.

Stefan Küng has been the lead developer for TortoiseSVN since the beginning. In addition to his open source work, Stefan has held senior positions in software and hardware design and engineering for over ten years. He holds a Master's Degree in Electrical Engineering from the Federal Institute of Technology in Zurich, Switzerland and is fluent in both German and English.

Eric Poole is the president and chief technology officer of RKT Technologies, Inc., a consulting and technical services company based in New Hampshire, USA. He has 40 years' experience in the industry, 35 year's experience as a software developer, and 31 years' experience as an independent consultant. RKT Technologies, Inc. specializes in software development and regulatory consulting for medical devices and other regulated industries. RKT's website can be seen at www.rkt-tech.com. Eric can be reached at eric@rkt-tech.com.

www.PacktPub.com

Support files, eBooks, discount offers and more

You might want to visit www.PacktPub.com for support files and downloads related to your book.

Did you know that Packt offers eBook versions of every book published, with PDF and ePub files available? You can upgrade to the eBook version at www.PacktPub.com and as a print book customer, you are entitled to a discount on the eBook copy. Get in touch with us at service@packtpub.com for more details.

At www.PacktPub.com, you can also read a collection of free technical articles, sign up for a range of free newsletters and receive exclusive discounts and offers on Packt books and eBooks.

http://PacktLib.PacktPub.com

Do you need instant solutions to your IT questions? PacktLib is Packt's online digital book library. Here, you can access, read and search across Packt's entire library of books.

Why Subscribe?

- ◆ Fully searchable across every book published by Packt
- ◆ Copy and paste, print and bookmark content
- ◆ On demand and accessible via web browser

Free Access for Packt account holders

If you have an account with Packt at www.PacktPub.com, you can use this to access PacktLib today and view nine entirely free books. Simply use your login credentials for immediate access.

Table of Contents

Preface

TortoiseSVN is a popular and easy-to-use Subversion client for Microsoft Windows. It is a Windows Shell extension, and is not limited to any particular IDE. TortoiseSVN is a free software which has been released under the GNU General Public License.

This book will help you to understand and use all of the features provided by TortoiseSVN. It will explain how to set up a Subversion server, and use TortoiseSVN for all of your source control needs. The book will begin with simple examples of source control, and then move on to more advanced scenarios and troubleshooting.

This book is based on the case study of a small software house called **Shiny Moose Software**. The company has a small team of developers, artists, and translators working on their software products. Some of the team are based in an office, others work from home.

Source control is important as a way to ensure that there are no conflicts or problems caused by different team members attempting to change the same file at the same time. It is also useful as a way of keeping track of changes made to individual files. You can see who changed a file, when they changed it, and what changes they made. You can even rewind time, and look at a snapshot of how a file was on a given date. TortoiseSVN is a good choice for Shiny Moose Software because it can be used by everyone from the developers and artists to the documentation writers.

What is Subversion?

Subversion is a version control system that solves the problem of multiple developers working on the same project. If you're accustomed to working alone, or in fairly small teams – just one or two people - you probably haven't encountered too many issues yet. This book will use the example of a small software house called Shiny Moose Software. The team has several members, and they often need to work on the same files. The team are currently working on **MooseHiragana**, a flash-card game to help people learn one of the Japanese alphabets.

The problem with sharing files

Let's imagine that Quinn, the manager at Shiny Moose Software, downloads the current version of the file called `questions.py`, and adds a few questions to it. At the same time, Mowbray notices that some of the existing flashcards are mapped incorrectly, so he also downloads the file and makes his corrections. Quinn uploads his changes, which took several hours to make, and then a few minutes later Mowbray uploads his version – wiping out all the work that Quinn has done.

If Shiny Moose Software had a decent version control system in place, this sort of thing wouldn't happen. Instead of work being lost because of two people editing the same file, edits can be prevented, or merged, depending on the type of version control in use.

Lock-modify-unlock

Some version control systems use lock-modify-unlock as a way of preventing problems. Under this system, Quinn would have been able to check out and lock `questions.py` when he started editing it. Mowbray would not be able to check out the file until Quinn was finished making his changes.

This system can work, but it has problems. What if Quinn forgets to upload his file, goes home, then gets sick and has to take time off work? Mowbray will have to get the systems administrator to unlock the file so that he can make his changes.

Also, it seems silly for Mowbray to be unable to correct a couple of mistakes at the beginning of the file when Quinn's edits aren't touching that content. That's where Subversion's **Copy-Modify-Merge** system comes in.

Copy-Modify-Merge

Under this system, which is the one that Subversion uses, Quinn and Mowbray are both able to work on the file at the same time. When they come to commit their changes, the second person to commit will be told that their file is out of date. They can then tell Subversion to look at what parts of the file have been changed, and merge the changes into the version in the repository. In the preceding example, where Quinn's and Mowbray's changes don't overlap, this works well, and neither team member will have to worry about what the other team member has been doing.

If Quinn and Mowbray had both edited the same part of the file, then a conflict would occur. In this case, the second person to commit would be told about the conflict, and they'd have to make a decision as to what they want to do – do they want to keep their changes, delete their changes, or manually copy over their team member's changes to resolve the conflict. Fortunately, TortoiseSVN makes it easy to see what's been going on in a file, so people can make informed decisions when a conflict arises.

You can see a diagram of the process as follows:

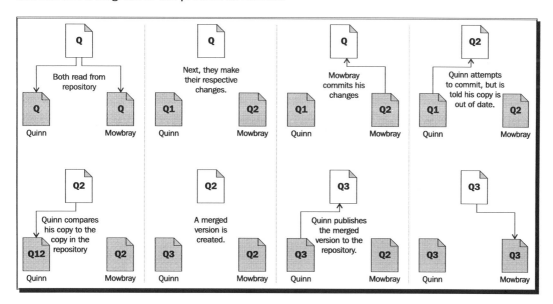

Locking is possible in Subversion, and can be useful in certain circumstances, but should not be used every time a file needs editing. No version control system is a substitute for good communication, but used in conjunction with a well organized team it can certainly make life a lot easier.

What this book covers

Chapter 1, Setting Up TortoiseSVN: This chapter will cover everything you need to know to get TortoiseSVN up and running. This chapter will explain how to install TortoiseSVN, and a Subversion server to use it with.

Chapter 2, Getting Started with TortoiseSVN: This chapter will explain the basic concepts that you will need to understand to work with a version control system, including creating working copies, and committing changes. You will learn how to use the repository browser, and how to perform basic tasks with TortoiseSVN.

Chapter 3, Creating and Applying Patches: This chapter explains how to create and apply patches, work with revision graphs, and use the Blame feature to keep track of who has made changes to your source code, and which lines they changed.

Chapter 4, Status Information and Conflicts: This chapter explains the different file statuses you may see when working with TortoiseSVN, and gives you tips on how to resolve the different kinds of file and tree conflicts.

Chapter 5: *Working with Revision Logs*: This chapter gives some examples of how to use revision graphs to document the development process of your application, how to change views, and how to perform simple maintenance tasks such as pruning trees.

Chapter 6, *Branching and Merging*: This chapter explains what branches can be used for, how to create a branch, how to switch your working copy, and how to merge branches and tress. This chapter will also explain how to track merges, and how to handle any conflicts which may arise.

Chapter 7, *Exporting and Relocating Working Copies*: This chapter shows you how to remove a working copy from version control – something you would need to do if you wanted to publish your source code on the web. You will also learn how to relocate your working copies. This knowledge is useful in case you ever need to change your SVN URL.

Chapter 8, *Keyword Substitution with SubWCRev*: This chapter will show you how to use SubWCRev to make keyword substitutions to a template file via the command-line, and how to automate the use of SubWCRev as a pre-build event in your IDE. This is useful for automatically changing certain text – for example the version number shown in your help files and about page.

Chapter 9, *Using TortoiseSVN with Bug Tracking Systems*: This chapter will give examples of how to use TortoiseSVN with popular bug tracking systems, including Trac, Google Projects, Redmine, and Jira.

Chapter 10, *Using SSL with TortoiseSVN*: This chapter will show you how create an OpenSSH certificate, how to create your public and private key pair, and how to use SVN+SSH with SVNServe and TortoiseSVN. SSH provides an extra layer of security for your SVN server.

Appendix A, *Command-line Reference*: This provides a quick reference guide to command-line switches for TortoiseSVN.

What you need for this book

TortoiseSVN will run on Windows 2000 SP2, Windows XP Service Pack 3, Windows Vista, and Windows 7. Both 32 and 64 bit OSes are supported.

Support for older versions of Windows (such as Windows 98 / ME / NT4) was dropped from TortoiseSVN in version 1.2.0, however older versions of TortoiseSVN are still available for download from the `http://tortoisesvn.net/` website. Subversion itself is backwards-compatible, so older clients can work with newer servers; however older clients are not able to work with working copies created by (or upgraded) using newer clients. If, for any reason, you run multiple clients on one machine, this is something that you will need to be aware of. This book is based on TortoiseSVN version 1.7.

SVNServe is an easy-to-deploy SVN Server. If you require more flexibility from your server, then you may prefer to use Apache and Subversion. Both solutions have minimal system requirements, and will support a small team of users even on older hardware.

TortoiseSVN can be used with any development environment.

Who this book is for

If you are a part of a development team that uses Subversion, and you carry out your work on a Windows-based computer, then this book is for you. No previous experience of version control software is required.

This book will help newcomers to source control learn everything they need to start using TortoiseSVN for team based software development. Those who have experience with other source-control systems will find the book useful as a primer to help them get up to speed with Subversion and TortoiseSVN.

Conventions

In this book, you will find several headings appearing frequently.

To give clear instructions of how to complete a procedure or task, we use:

Time for action – heading

1. Action 1

2. Action 2

3. Action 3

Instructions often need some extra explanation so that they make sense, so they are followed with:

What just happened?

This heading explains the working of tasks or instructions that you have just completed.

You will also find some other learning aids in the book, including:

Pop quiz – heading

These are short multiple choice questions intended to help you test your own understanding.

Have a go hero – heading

These set practical challenges and give you ideas for experimenting with what you have learned.

You will also find a number of styles of text that distinguish between different kinds of information. Here are some examples of these styles, and an explanation of their meaning.

Code words in text are shown as follows: "Mowbray, while working on the branch, renames `hiscore.py` to `scoring.py` and commits it to the repository."

New terms and **important words** are shown in bold. Words that you see on the screen, in menus or dialog boxes for example, appear in the text like this: " The **Merge** dialog will appear. "

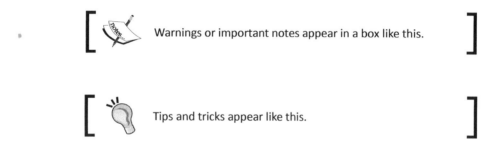

Warnings or important notes appear in a box like this.

Tips and tricks appear like this.

Reader feedback

Feedback from our readers is always welcome. Let us know what you think about this book —what you liked or may have disliked. Reader feedback is important for us to develop titles that you really get the most out of.

To send us general feedback, simply send an e-mail to `feedback@packtpub.com`, and mention the book title via the subject of your message.

If there is a book that you need and would like to see us publish, please send us a note in the **SUGGEST A TITLE** form on `www.packtpub.com` or e-mail `suggest@packtpub.com`.

If there is a topic that you have expertise in and you are interested in either writing or contributing to a book, see our author guide on `www.packtpub.com/authors`.

Customer support

Now that you are the proud owner of a Packt book, we have a number of things to help you to get the most from your purchase.

Errata

Although we have taken every care to ensure the accuracy of our content, mistakes do happen. If you find a mistake in one of our books—maybe a mistake in the text or the code—we would be grateful if you would report this to us. By doing so, you can save other readers from frustration and help us improve subsequent versions of this book. If you find any errata, please report them by visiting http://www.packtpub.com/support, selecting your book, clicking on the **errata submission form** link, and entering the details of your errata. Once your errata are verified, your submission will be accepted and the errata will be uploaded on our website, or added to any list of existing errata, under the Errata section of that title. Any existing errata can be viewed by selecting your title from http://www.packtpub.com/support.

Piracy

Piracy of copyright material on the Internet is an ongoing problem across all media. At Packt, we take the protection of our copyright and licenses very seriously. If you come across any illegal copies of our works, in any form on the Internet, please provide us with the location address or website name immediately so that we can pursue a remedy.

Please contact us at copyright@packtpub.com with a link to the suspected pirated material.

We appreciate your help in protecting our authors, and our ability to bring you valuable content.

Questions

You can contact us at questions@packtpub.com if you are having a problem with any aspect of the book, and we will do our best to address it.

1

Setting up TortoiseSVN

__TortoiseSVN__ is a free and open-source Subversion client for Microsoft Windows. It is not tied to any particular __Integrated Development Environment (IDE)__; instead, it is a shell extension which integrates into the Windows Explorer, giving you easy access to Subversion repositories from within applications you're already familiar with. This means that it can be used with any software, and by all members of your development team.

In this chapter, you will learn how to set up TortoiseSVN, and how to set up a Subversion server to use it with. You will also learn a little bit about the TortoiseSVN user interface, so that you have an idea of the basic options provided by the software. Later chapters will explore each of those options in detail.

In this chapter, we shall:

- Install TortoiseSVN
- Create a repository
- Install **SVNserve** – a simple, easy-to-set-up Subversion server
- Install Apache + Subversion – a more flexible Subversion server

So let's get on with it...

Choosing your TortoiseSVN version

The first thing you need to do is choose the right version of TortoiseSVN for your computer. TortoiseSVN is available in two versions, one for 32-bit versions of Windows, and one for 64-bit versions of Windows. The 32-bit version can be used on both 32 and 64 bit versions of Windows, allowing you to use Subversion with older 32-bit applications on more modern operating systems, while the 64-bit version will work on 64-bit versions of Windows only.

You may already know which version you need, in which case, you can skip this section and go straight on to *Installing TortoiseSVN*. However if you aren't sure what flavor of Windows your computer is running, follow the below instructions to identify which version you need.

Checking your operating system edition

If you aren't sure whether you're running a 64-bit or 32-bit version of Windows, you can check quite easily. If you didn't install the operating system yourself, it's a good idea to double check. Remember that it's possible to run a 32-bit operating system on a 64-bit processor and it's not uncommon for department stores to sell pre-built computers with a 32-bit operating system, even if the processor powering the computer is a 64-bit one.

Time for action – checking Windows Vista / 7's architecture

To check the architecture of a Windows Vista or Windows 7 computer, follow these steps:

1. Click the **Start** button.

2. Click inside the **Start Search** box.

3. Type `msinfo32.exe` and then press the *Enter* key.

4. A **System Information** window should appear. Look in the right-hand pane for **System Type**. If you have a 32-bit version of Windows, the **System Type** will be **x86-based PC**. If you have a 64-bit version of Windows, the **System Type** will be **x64-based PC**.

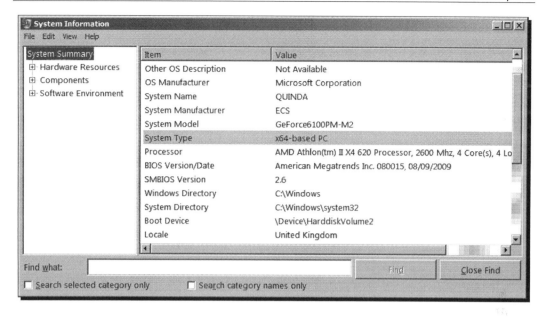

What just happened?

You have now identified the architecture of your Windows Vista or Windows 7 computer's operating system. Armed with this knowledge, you will be able to make the correct decision as to which version of TortoiseSVN to download.

Time for action – checking Windows XP's architecture

To check the architecture of a Windows XP computer, follow these steps:

1. Click the **Start** button.

2. Click **Run...**

3. In the box that appears, type `winmsd.exe` and then hit the *Enter* key.

4. A **System Information** window should appear. Look in the right-hand pane for **System Type**. If you have a 32-bit version of Windows, the **System Type** will be **x86-based PC**. If you have a 64-bit version of Windows, the **System Type** will be **x64-based PC**.

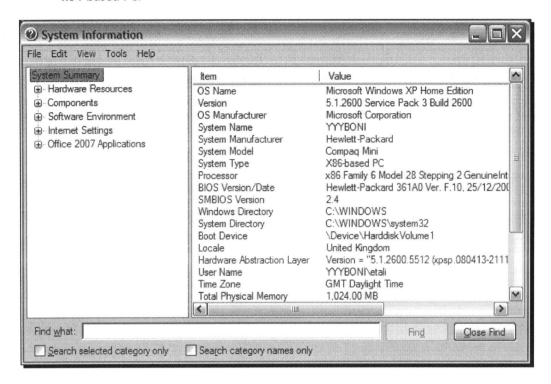

What just happened?

You have now identified the architecture of your computer's XP based operating system. You can use this knowledge to choose the correct version (or versions) of TortoiseSVN for your computer.

Time for action – checking Windows Server 2003 architecture

To check the architecture of a Windows Server 2003 based computer, follow these steps:

1. Click the **Start** button.

2. Click **Run**.

3. In the box that appears, type `sysadm.cpl` and then press the *Enter* key.

4. On the **General** tab of the window that appears, you should see **Microsoft(R) Windows (R) Server 2003, Enterprise Edition** if you are running the 32-bit edition. If you are running the 64-bit edition, you will see **Microsoft(R) Windows (R) Server 2003 Enterprise x64 Edition**.

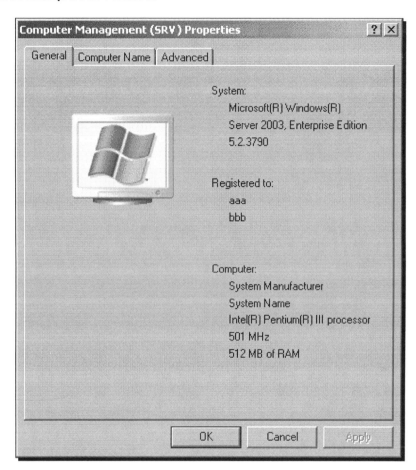

What just happened?

You have just identified the architecture of the version of Windows that is installed on your computer. It is important to know whether you are running a 32-bit or 64-bit operating system so that we can install the correct version of TortoiseSVN.

If you have a 32-bit version of Windows, you should install the 32-bit version of TortoiseSVN. If you have a 64-bit version of Windows, you can install both the 32-bit and 64-bit versions of TortoiseSVN side-by-side. Doing this will enable TortoiseSVN's features for both 32-bit and 64-bit applications.

Why is 32-bit called x86?

You may be wondering why 64-bit is called x64, but 32-bit is called x86. The reason is part of the history of computing. x86 is a CPU instruction set which is used in most modern processors. There are three subsets of the x86 instruction set – x86-16 (16 bit), x86-32 (32-bit), and x86-64 (64-bit). The 32-bit version of the x86 instruction set was first used in the 80386 processor, and quickly became an industry standard.

The term x86 really refers to backwards compatibility with the original 8086 instruction set, but the popularity of the x86-32 subset means that most people use the term x86 to refer to a modern 32-bit processor.

Installing TortoiseSVN

Now that you know which version of TortoiseSVN you need, it's time to download and install it. The good news is TortoiseSVN is a small download, and has an easy-to-use installer.

Administrator privileges needed

You will need Administrator privileges to install TortoiseSVN. Most home computers run with the default user being the admin user, but if you are following this book at work, you may need to request assistance from your company's IT department.

Time for action – installing TortoiseSVN

1. Go to http://www.Tortoisesvn.net, and click the **Download** link in the sidebar at the left-hand side of the screen.

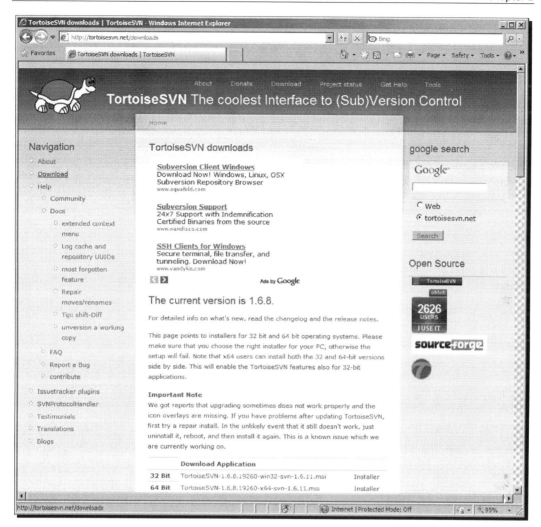

2. If you have a 32-bit version of Windows, download the **32 Bit** version of the installer. Users of 64-bit windows can download both the **32 Bit** and **the 64 Bit** versions, although in most cases only the 64-bit version will be required. The 32-bit version is needed only if you want TortoiseSVN to work with legacy applications.

3. Once the download completes, right-click on the `.msi` file, select **Properties**, navigate to the **Digital Signatures** tab and confirm that the signature is present. It should look something like the following screenshot:

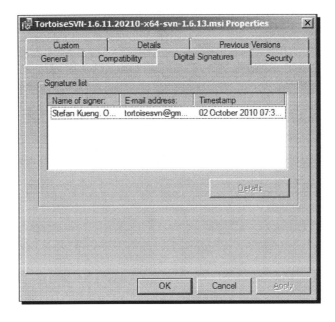

4. Next, double-click on the install file to run it.

5. Depending on the version of Windows you have, you may see a security warning similar to the one shown in the next screenshot. If the warning appears, click **Run** to dismiss it and continue with the installation.

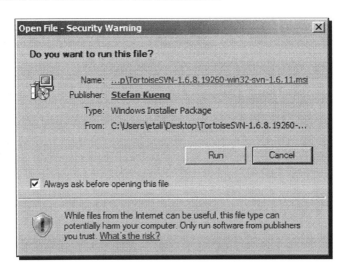

6. When the installer welcome screen appears, click **Next**.

7. Read the license agreement. If you agree to the terms, select **I accept the terms of the License Agreement** and click **Next**.

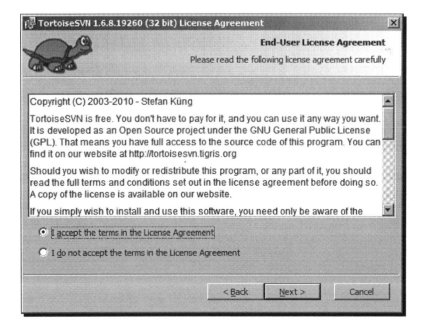

In most cases, the default options presented on the **Custom Setup** screen will be acceptable. If you do not want the additional icons, or one of the dictionaries, you can remove them by clicking on the down arrow next to the relevant option, and then clicking the red cross next to **Entire feature will be unavailable**. I recommend you leave **Register diff/patch files** checked, as this will ensure that TortoiseUDiff is set as the default for opening `.diff` and `.patch` files. Once you are happy with the list of features, click **Next**.

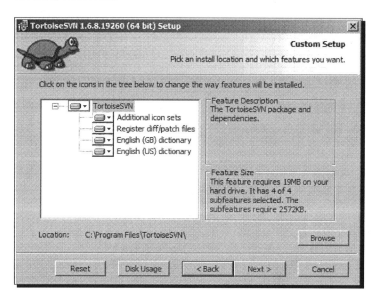

8. Next, click **Install**.

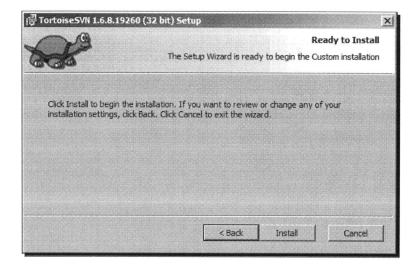

Depending on the speed of your computer, the installation may take a few minutes. When it completes, you should see a window similar to the one shown in the following screenshot:

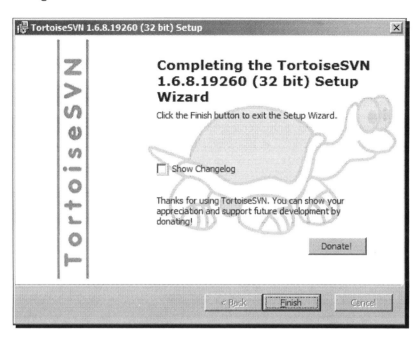

9. After clicking **Finish**, you will be prompted to reboot. Click **Yes** if you are ready to reboot, or click **No** if you need to save some work or close some applications before rebooting. Make sure you do reboot before using TortoiseSVN.

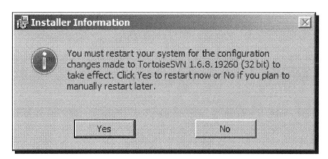

What just happened?

We have just installed TortoiseSVN. Remember that if you have a 64-bit version of Windows, you can use both the 32-bit and 64-bit versions side-by-side if required. So, if you have just installed the 32-bit version, don't forget to install the 64-bit version. The installation process is the same for both versions. In most cases, users of 64-bit versions of Windows will be fine with the 64-bit version of TortoiseSVN. However, if you find that some of your older applications lack the context menu functionality of TortoiseSVN, then it's likely that they are 32-bit applications, and therefore need the 32-bit version of TortoiseSVN to be installed.

The effects of the installation may not be obvious. The most obvious change is that you now have some new right-click options – try right-clicking on a text file on your hard drive to see the options that TortoiseSVN has added. We will be exploring a few of these options later on in this chapter. The new right-click options are shown in the following screenshot:

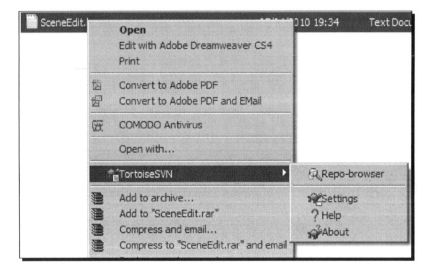

The right-click menu is context sensitive – right-clicking a folder, for example, will give different options to right-clicking a file. Right-clicking on a shortcut, or multiple files at once, will also give different options. We will explore these in greater depth later.

Language packs and spellchecking

TortoiseSVN has been translated into several different languages. You can see a list of the available language packs at: `http://tortoisesvn.net/downloads`.

The language packs are offered as executable installers. Simply download the ones you need, double-click the file to execute it, and follow the on-screen instructions.

TortoiseSVN also comes with a spellchecking feature, which allows you to check the spelling of commit log messages. The installer automatically sets up the British English and American English language files, however some people may need to spell check using different languages –for example, Australian English differs slightly from British English and American English.

Time for action – adding new spellchecking dictionaries

1. Download the dictionary of your choice (for example, English (Australian)) from `http://wiki.services.openoffice.org/wiki/Dictionaries`.

2. Extract the `.zip` file, and look at the file names – they should match the standard formatting of `language_COUNTRY` – for example `en_AU.aff` and `en_AU.dic` – if there are extra characters or words in the file name, remove them.

Copy the files to the `/bin/` folder inside your TortoiseSVN installation. Restart TortoiseSVN – your dictionary should be available for use.

What just happened?

You have installed an extra dictionary for spell-checking purposes. When you install a new language, the spell-checking functionality for that language is installed alongside it. However, it is possible to install spell-check dictionaries separately. This is useful for people who live in a country, who speak a dialect not covered by the standard TortoiseSVN language files.

Now, when you go to submit a changelog, spell-checking will be enabled.

If you have more than one dictionary installed, you can select the one you want to use via the **Project Language** option in the **Project Settings** menu – we will explore those options in more detail later.

Creating a repository

Now that you have our client installed, you can make a repository. This is where the master copy of the code that we are working on (and any previous versions of the code) will be stored. You can then import code into the repository. Before we make any changes to the code, we will have to create a "working copy" of the code – this is useful because it helps if something goes wrong and a developer breaks the "working copy", there will still be a functional copy in the repository, which the developer can re-download.

Time for action – creating a repository

1. Create a new folder on your **C:** drive. If you're using Windows XP, create the folder in C:\svn_repository. Users of Windows Vista or 7 should create the folder under their user folder.

2. Navigate to that folder, right-click inside it, and then from the **TortoiseSVN** menu, select **Create repository here**.

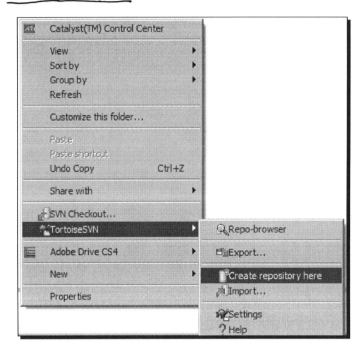

3. After a couple of seconds, you should see a message saying that the repository was successfully created, and several files and folders should appear inside the repository folder.

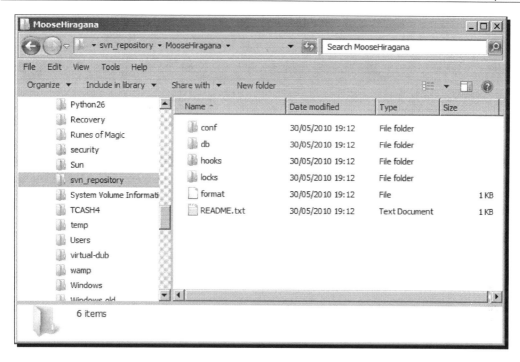

4. Congratulations, you've made your first repository!

What just happened?

You've just set up a repository. This is a central location where the code for your software projects is stored. In *Chapter 2, Getting Started With TortoiseSVN*, you will learn how to check out code from this repository, so that you can work on it – uploading your changes once you are done. The copy that you have checked out is called the "Working Copy" because it is the copy you are directly working on – not because of the status of the code!

The repository will keep track of each version, so if you make a change today and then decide later on that the change was a bad idea, you can roll back to a version of the code that existed before you made the undesired change.

Before we explore those features, it's a good idea to organize the repository so that it's easy to work with in the future.

There are a couple of different ways of organizing a repository. If you're planning on having only one project in the repository, you can get away with creating three top-level directories to handle branches, tags, and the trunk.

If you will be hosting more than one project within your repository, then you should create a folder for each project, and then put the `branches`, `tags`, and `trunk` folders in there, shown as follows:

```
MooseHirigana
        /branches
        /tags
        /trunk

Project2
        /branches

        /tags

        /trunk

Project3
        /branches

        /tags

        /trunk
```

The above layout is just an example. Subversion itself does not care what layout you use. If you have a different idea for the folder layout, then you can use that. The most important thing is that the layout is consistently enforced, and understood by all the members of your team.

Create your chosen folder structure in a temporary folder on your hard drive, then right-click on the folder and select **TortoiseSVN | Import** to import the structure to your new repository.

Now let's set up a Subversion server so that other members of the team at Shiny Moose Software can take advantage of the features that Subversion offers.

Time for action – testing your repository

Now that you've made your repository, it's time to check that you can access it.

1. Create a new folder that you will use to as your working area while you are developing your application. You can place the folder anywhere you wish. For ease of access, I placed it on my desktop.

2. Right-click inside that folder, and select **SVN checkout**.

3. Click on the **...** button next to the URL of repository option, and browse to the path of your repository.

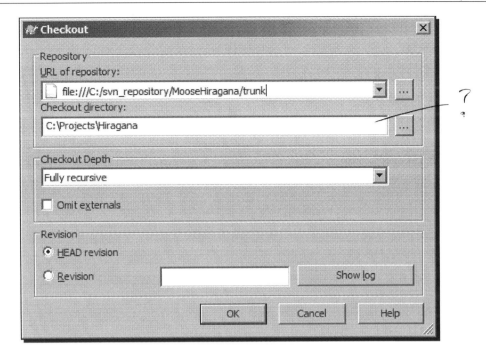

4. Notice that the local path is formatted like this: `file:///C:/svn_repository/` `MooseHiragana` - the UNIX-style slashes, and the `file:///` notation is important – Windows-style slashes won't work.

5. Click **OK**.

6. View the working folder again; you should see a **Hiragana** folder inside it. The folder icon should have a small green tick. The tick means that the copy's status is "Normal".

Setting up the SVNServe server

To make full use of your Subversion client, you need a Subversion server. It is possible to run the client and the server on the same machine, although for larger development teams, a stand-alone server will offer better performance.

The simplest way to set up a Subversion server is to use SVNServe. This method generally provides good performance too. I recommend that you use an SVNServe-based server unless you require some of the more advanced features offered by an Apache and Subversion-based server.

Time for action – setting up SVNServe

1. Download the **CollabNet Subversion Server** and client for Windows from `http://www.collab.net/downloads/subversion` - you will need to create an account to do this, but don't worry, registration on **CollabNet** is free, and they won't share your e-mail address with anyone.

2. Run the installer, and follow the on-screen instructions. As we want SVNServe only, deselect the **Apache(MOD_DAV_SVN)** option and click **Next**.

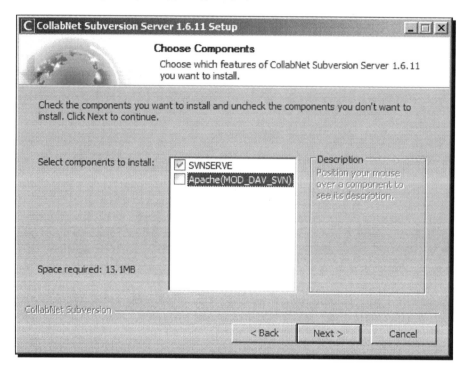

3. Ensure that the **Install svnserve to run as a Windows service** option is checked. For most people, the default Port is OK. Choose a **Repository Path** which matches the path you created for your repositories in the previous "Time For Action". In the case of Shiny Moose Software, the default path is correct.

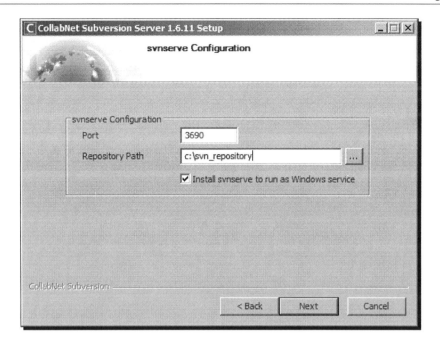

4. In most cases, the options on the **Automatic Updates** screen can be left at the defaults. If you use a proxy to connect to the internet (which is unlikely, unless you are installing the server in an office environment), then tick the relevant box, and fill out the proxy details when prompted.

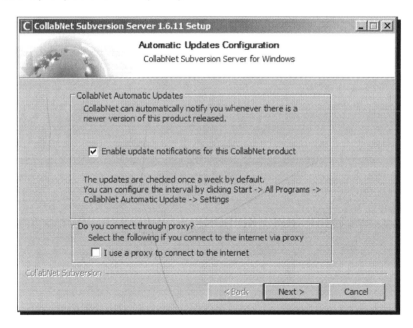

5. Finally, click **Finish**.

What just happened?

We have just set up a simple SVNServe-based Subversion server. At the moment, we can't do much with the server. It allows anonymous read access, but no write access. That means it's great for letting people download our code, but not so useful for letting people submit any changes they decide to make.

We could allow anonymous write access – but that wouldn't really be a good idea – after all, what's to stop a competitor, or simply a mean-spirited person, from changing our code? Also, how will you know which member of your team submitted which changes? Giving each user of your repository a username makes it a lot easier to track who is doing what, and also to restrict what each person can do. Instead of allowing anonymous write access, let's set up some simple authentication, so that we can control who can and cannot edit our code.

Simple authentication for SVNserve

SVNserve has a simple authentication feature which allows you to specify who can and cannot modify code in the repository. Let's set up that feature now.

Time for action – setting up simple authentication for SVNserve

1. Navigate to the /conf/ folder in your repository, and open svnserve.conf.

2. Paste the following lines underneath the line that says [general].

```
anon-access = none
auth-access = write
password-db = users
```

3. Save the file, and create a new file called users (with no extension) in the same folder.

4. Drag the users file over a Notepad window to edit it, and enter the following text (where **AUSERNAME** is any username and **APASSWORD** is the password you want that user to have:

```
[users]
AUSERNAME = APASSWORD
```

What just happened?

You have set up your Subversion server so that unauthenticated users cannot access the server, and authenticated users can read from and write to the server.

The code we added to the `config` file in step 2 tells SVNserve that anonymous access is not permitted, and that authorized users (those listed in the users file) should have write access to the repository.

Have a go hero – adding more users and repositories

Now that you know how to make a repository, and how to set up some security, why not try making a new repository, and using different login details for it. Imagine that Shiny Moose Software decides to produce a second game called GermanMoose – they want to give the same people who are working on the Hiragana game access to the GermanMoose repository, but they also want to give a new employee, called Dieter, access to that repository so that he can work on translations.

Create a new repository, and make a copy of the users file, with a username and password for Dieter added to it. Check that you can access the folder with the right permissions.

Setting up an Apache + Subversion server

An Apache and Subversion-based server is a more flexible (and more complicated) Subversion solution. It is up to you whether you choose to use this setup. If you are happy with the functionality and performance of a SVNserve-based setup, then it would be wise to use that instead.

An Apache and Subversion-based setup is useful if you want to allow users to browse your repository via a web browser, or if you want to use SSL encryption for extra security. Another benefit of Apache and Subversion is that your server can use any authentication method that Apache supports.

If you do not need any of those features, then you may prefer SVNserve as it is easier to deploy and manage, and also performs slightly faster in most cases. By far the easiest way to set up an Apache server on Windows is to use VisualSVN, a combined installer for Apache, VisualSVN, and an administrative panel.

Time for action – installing VisualSVN

1. Download VisualSVN from `http://www.visualsvn.com/server/download`.

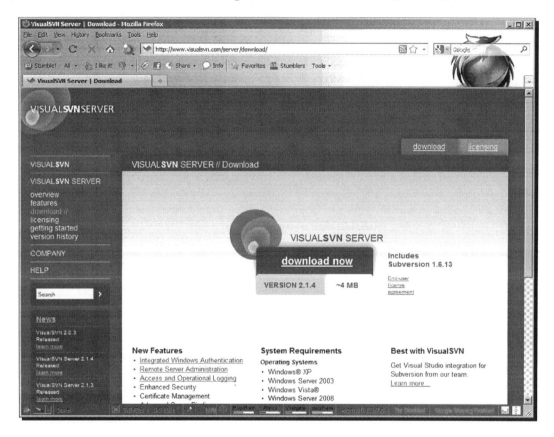

2. Run the installer, and click **Next** when prompted.

3. Set the path for your repository. Windows XP users can accept the defaults. Windows Vista and Windows 7 users may need to change the repository folder path to one inside their user directory.

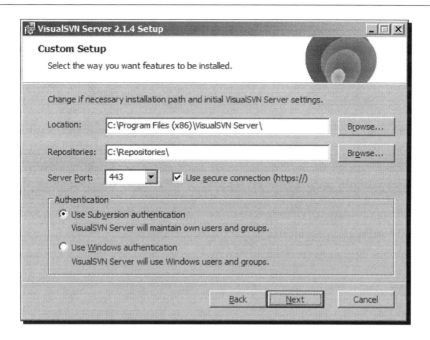

4. Once the installation is done, you should see a window which looks like the following screenshot:

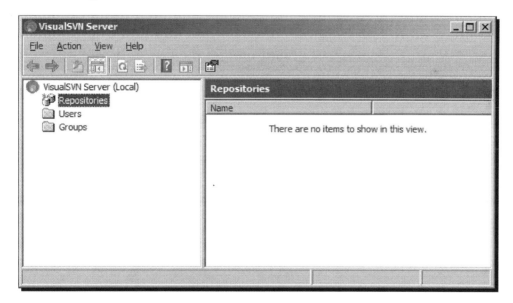

5. You can create a new repository by going to **Action | Create New Repository**, and entering the name of the repository there.

What just happened?

You have just installed VisualSVN. This offers an easy-to-use management console, and gives you a working Subversion server right out of the box. The default setup is ready-to-go, but there are some extra features you will want to look at if you're using the server in a production environment.

You will find a full guide to the more advanced features of VisualSVN, such as SSL, at `http://www.visualsvn.com/server/getting-started/`.

VisualSVN is the quickest and easiest way to get a working Subversion server. This method is the best choice for most people.

For the sake of completeness, the following instructions explain how to set up Apache and Subversion separately. If you are using VisualSVN, you can skip the rest of the sections in this chapter.

Time for action – installing Apache

1. Download Apache from: `http://httpd.apache.org/download.cgi`. I recommend you choose the newest stable binary installer that includes OpenSSL. You will find the Windows installers under **Other Files | Binaries | Win32**.

2. Run the installer, and follow the on-screen instructions.

3. For the **Server Information**, enter a descriptive **Network Domain** and **Server Name**. If you will be using Subversion on your local network, I recommend you use a domain name ending in `.local`. If you want your server to be accessible over the internet, you will need to use a valid domain.

4. Leave the radio button that says **for All Users, on Port 80, as a Service --Recommended** selected, as shown in the following screenshot:

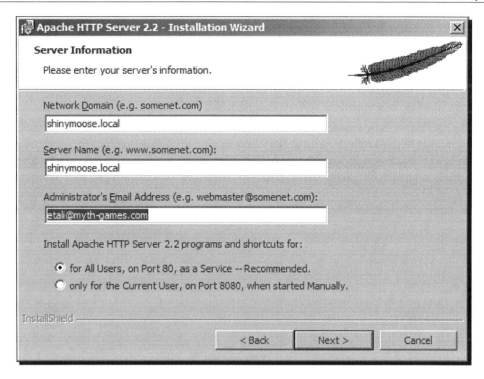

5. On the next screen, choose **Typical install**, then click **Next**.

6. Select a path to install Apache to (for most people, the default will be fine), then click **Next**.

7. Depending on the speed of your computer, the installation process may take several minutes.

8. To confirm that Apache is installed correctly, open your web browser and go to `http://localhost`, you should see a screen containing a message saying **It works!**, as follows:

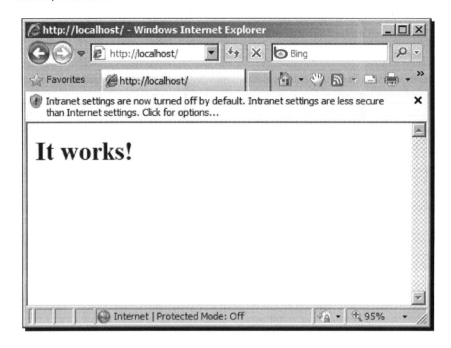

What just happened?

You have successfully installed the Apache web server for Windows. The **It works!** page you viewed in your web browser may not look impressive, but is a simple HTML web page!

The Apache server will be used by Subversion to allow users to access your repositories over the network (or the internet, if you choose to set your firewall up to allow that) using a web browser.

Time for action – installing Subversion

1. Download Subversion from `http://subversion.tigris.org/servlets/Proj ectDocumentList?folderID=8100` – make sure you select the correct version of Subversion for your Apache installation.

2. Install Subversion, and follow the on-screen instructions.

3. If Subversion detected Apache, skip to step nine. If it did not, follow steps 4-8.

4. Go to `c:\Program Files\Subversion`, and open the `\httpd` folder. Copy `mod_dav_svn.so` and `mod_authz_svn.so` to `c:\Program Files\Apache Group\apache2\modules`

5. Go to `c:\Program Files\Subversion\bin` and copy `libdb44.dll` and `int13_svn.dll` from that folder to Apache's `\bin` directory.

6. Open Apache's `httpd.conf` file in Notepad, or your favorite programmer's text editor. You can find the file at `c:\Program Files\Apache Group\Apache2\conf\`

7. Uncomment the following two lines by removing the # sign at the beginning of them:

```
#LoadModule dav_fs_module modules/mod_dav_fs.so
#LoadModule dav_module modules/mod_dav.so
```

By uncommenting the preceding lines, we are telling Apache to load the `mod_dav` modules.

8. Add the following two lines to the end of the **LoadModule** section in `http.conf`:

```
LoadModule dav_svn_module modules/mod_dav_svn.so
LoadModule authz_svn_module modules/mod_authz_svn.so
```

9. Open `httpd.conf`, and at the end of the file, add the following:

```
<Location /svn>
DAV svn
SVNListParentPath on
SVNParentPath c:\svn_repository
AuthType Basic
AuthName "Subversion repositories"
AuthUserFile passwd
Require valid-user
</Location>
```

The preceding code tells apache to use Basic Auth security on the `/svn` folder, and tells it where to find the file containing the usernames and passwords. Basic Auth is a simple form of security where a user is prompted by their browser for a username and password when they navigate to a protected folder. Basic Auth is not encrypted, so is not suitable for protecting areas which contain sensitive data.

10. Finally, open a command prompt (**Start | Run | CMD**), navigate to the `c:\Program Files\Apache Group\Apache2.2` folder, and enter:

`bin\htpasswd -c passwd USERNAME`

Where USERNAME is the user ID you plan to use to access the Subversion server.

11. When prompted, enter a password for that user.

12. Now you should be able to access your Subversion server by navigating to http://localhost/svn in your web browser – enter the username and password when prompted:

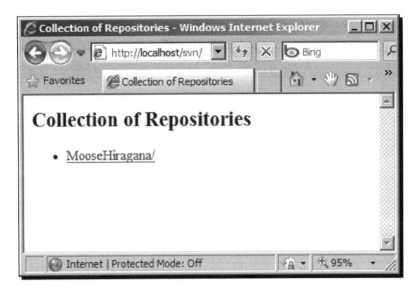

What just happened?

You have just created a basic example of an Apache + Subversion server. From here you can add extra security with SASL Authentication and Encryption.

An Apache + Subversion server setup is useful for developers who want more robust authentication, and the ability to allow access to their repository via the web.

The basic authentication should be sufficient for an internal server. You can have as many users as you want. Each employee at Shiny Moose Software has their own login details, which makes it easy for the lead developer to see who is working on which part of the program, and what changes they have made.

Adding more users

You can add more users to the server by using the command: `bin\htpasswd passwd USERNAME`. This will allow you to give each member of your team their own user ID and password, so that you can keep track of who has changed which file, and what changes they made.

Pop quiz – subversion concepts

1. The 32-bit version of TortoiseSNV

   a. Comes on 32 floppy discs.

   b. Is used on 32-bit Windows and on 64-bit Windows by 32-bit applications.

   c. Is able to handle only 32 repositories at once.

2. A "working copy"

   a. Is a copy of the source code that still works.

   b. Is an illegal copy of your source code that is being downloaded by software pirates.

   c. Is the copy that you have checked out of the repository.

3. Apache and Subversion

   a. Is used by people who prefer Apaches to Tortoises.

   b. Is more flexible and offers more security options, but is harder to set up than SVNserve.

   c. Is easy to set up, but offers fewer options than SVNserve.

Summary

This chapter focused on setting up TortoiseSVN and a Subversion server for it to be used with.

Specifically, we covered:

♦ Identifying which TortoiseSVN version you need – the 32-bit version is designed for 32-bit Windows installs, and also works with 32-bit applications on 64-bit Windows installs. The 64-bit version can only be used on 64-bit Windows installs, and with 64-bit applications.

♦ Installing TortoiseSVN.

- Installing SVNserve – an easy-to-install and effective Subversion server, this runs as a Windows Service.

- Installing Apache and Subversion – a more sophisticated way to run a Subversion server.

We also touched on securing your server – we will explore that in more detail in *Chapter 9, Using SSH With TortoiseSVN*.

So far, you have installed TortoiseSVN and used it to create a repository. You have also set up a server, so that each member of your team can access the repository. You may be wondering when you will get to see TortoiseSVN in action – well, the good news is that you don't have to wait any longer – *Chapter 2, Getting Started With TortoiseSVN* will give you your first taste of using TortoiseSVN – you will learn how to use the repository browser, check out a Working Copy, and commit any changes you made to the copy.

2
Getting Started With TortoiseSVN

*In this chapter you will get your first taste of using TortoiseSVN. This chapter will explain the concept of working copies and will cover how to check out a **working copy**, how to manage **copy depth,** and how to **commit** a copy after you have made some changes to it. This process is the nuts-and-bolts of version management and something that you will be doing a lot during your work with TortoiseSVN.*

In this chapter we shall:

- ◆ Learn the benefits of using a working copy
- ◆ Learn how to check out a working copy and how to check in after making changes
- ◆ See some of the more common **commit log messages** and learn what they mean
- ◆ Explore the repository browser

So let's get on with it...

Our case study

Shiny Moose Software is a software house with a small team of developers. They have just started working on their first project—a Hiragana Learning Game written in Python. The lead developer, Quinn, has created a skeleton for the project. He has written the code for the games "splash screen".

One of the other developers, Mowbray, downloaded a compressed archive containing Quinn's code and found that on his older computer, the CPU usage spiked massively when the code was run. He looked at the code and noticed that Quinn had made a poor choice when deciding how to detect mouse events. The problem is simple to fix, but Mowbray knows that communicating the changes to Quinn could be problematic.

Mowbray could make the required changes and then e-mail the updated code to Quinn, but what if Quinn returns to his computer and resumes his work on the application before he checks his e-mail? What if one of the other developers at Shiny Moose Software has also decided to make some changes to the code? Keeping track of changes submitted by several different developers would be confusing enough even with this relatively small application. Imagine how difficult it would become when the code is measured in hundreds, or thousands of lines, rather than just a few dozen!

This is where Subversion saves the day. Instead of copying the code from a normal shared folder, or downloading it from the company's intranet site, Mowbray can use TortoiseSVN to **check out** a **working copy** of the code, inform the Subversion server that is currently working on that file, make the changes, and check it back in.

A word about our examples

The code snippets used in this book are incredibly simplistic. Please don't use them as examples for how to write a Python application! Also, don't worry too much about the language or IDE used in these examples. TortoiseSVN can be used with any language and any development environment. Even team members working on other areas, such as documentation or translation work, can take advantage of TortoiseSVN. The most important thing is to understand the version control principles which are being applied.

Working copies explained

The first thing Mowbray needs to do is check out a working copy. He can make changes to this copy and then submit the changes once he is done.

Time for action – checking out a working copy

Checking out a working copy takes just a few simple steps.

1. Create a folder which you will use to store your working copies. For example, `C:\Projects\MooseHiragana`.

2. Right-click inside that folder and select **SVN Checkout...** from the menu that appears.

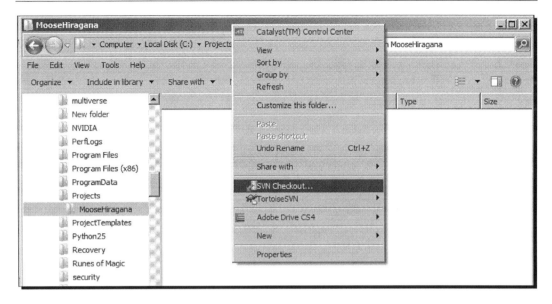

3. Browse to your project's repository (or enter the correct network path) and click **OK**.

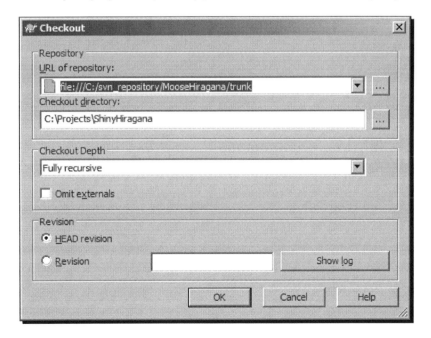

4. A window containing a list of the files which have been checked out will appear.

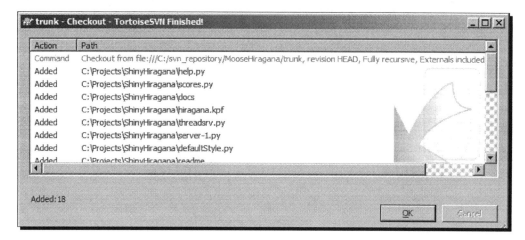

5. If the checkout was successful, you should see a list of files in your chosen directory, with a green tick on the icon of each file.

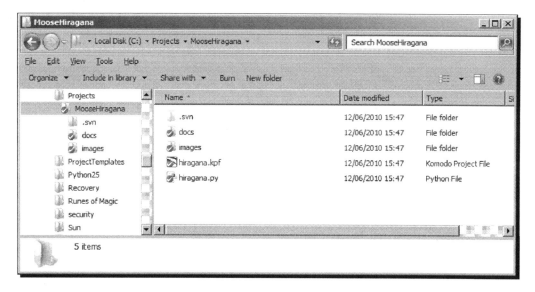

What just happened?

You have just checked out a working copy of the files which are stored on the repository. This is useful because it allows you to safely test, change, and experiment with the code without the risk of breaking the original code.

Once you are happy with the changes you have made, you can check them in to the repository, so that your fellow developers can synchronize their copies to see your changes.

Local repositories vs. remote repositories

Throughout this book, we will use remote repositories in most of our examples. It is likely that you will, at some point, need to work with a remote repository—either one which is accessed via the internet, or one which is part of your company's network. In that case, all you need to do is enter the full network/internet address of the repository in the place of the `file:///` reference in the URL of Repository box.

Checkout depth

The **MooseHiragana** project is quite small, so there is no issue with checking out the entire repository. If you were working on a much larger project, which had thousands of files, then you may prefer to save time, bandwidth and storage space by checking out only the folders that relate to the part of the project you are working on.

Time for action – using checkout depth

1. Using a different folder for this working copy, right-click inside the folder, and select **SVN Checkout...**.

2. This time, in the **Checkout** window that appears, as well as selecting the correct repository, choose **Only file children** from the **Checkout Depth** dropdown.

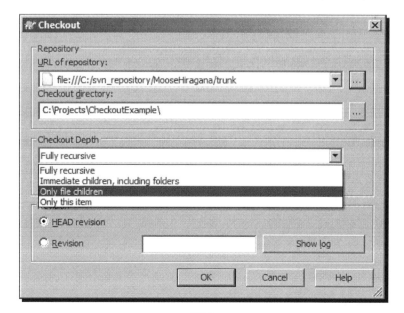

3. You should see that when the checkout process completes, all the files that are part of the root folder appear in your working copy, but none of the folders have been checked out.

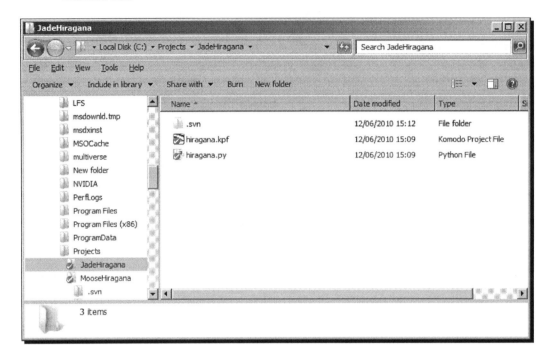

What just happened?

You have just checked out only the files that are in the root folder of the project on the Subversion server. That may not seem like a particularly useful feature when the project consists of just a few files, but imagine if there were thousands of files.

The `checkout depth` feature becomes useful when projects increase greatly in size. It is also useful if your team has members that work only on specific parts of the application. For example, an artist could check out only the images folder, or a translator could check out only the folder containing the localization files for the language he is working in. If the artist then needs to expand his checkout to include deeper folders, he can use the repository browser to select the extra folders that he needs.

There are a number of different **checkout depth** options. The following table explains what each option means.

Checkout Depth Option	Purpose
Fully recursive	Checks out the entire tree, including all child folders and sub-folders.
Immediate children, including folders	Checks out the specified directory, including all files and child folders, but does not populate the child folders.
Only file children	Checks out the specified directory, including all files, but does not check out any child folders.
Only this item	Checks out the selected directory only. Does not populate it with files or child folders.
Working copy	This option is not shown on the **checkout** dialog, but it is the default for all other dialogs which have a depth setting. This option tells TortoiseSVN to adhere to the depth specified in the working copy.
Exclude	This option is not shown on the **checkout** dialog. It is used to reduce the depth of the working copy after a folder has already been populated.

Have a go hero – working with checkout depth

Imagine that you are an artist. You have been hired by Shiny Moose Software and asked to redesign the logo used on the splash screen and also to create a smaller one for use in the theme of the game.

The directory structure chosen by the developers looks like this:

The images that you will be working on are stored in the **/images** folder. You will not need to work on anything inside the **/images/artwork** or **/images/japanese** folders.

You need to set up your working copy. Rather than cluttering your filesystem with files that you will never need to use, you have decided to checkout only the folder you need for your work—the **/images** folder.

Using another user account (or another PC on your network), try checking out just the contents of that folder from the repository. If you prefer, you could simply create a new working directory using the same user. However, if you do this, you should note that any changes made in that folder will be marked with your own user name. That may be fine for testing TortoiseSVN's features, but is not good practice in a production environment.

Committing changes to a repository

Now that Mowbray has checked out a working copy of the MooseHiragana source code, he can change the source code to fix the speed issue he noticed and then commit the changes to the repository.

Time for action – committing changes to a repository

1. After you have finished editing the files that you want to change in the project, save the files and open the project folder. You should see a red exclamation mark on the icon of any files that have been changed.

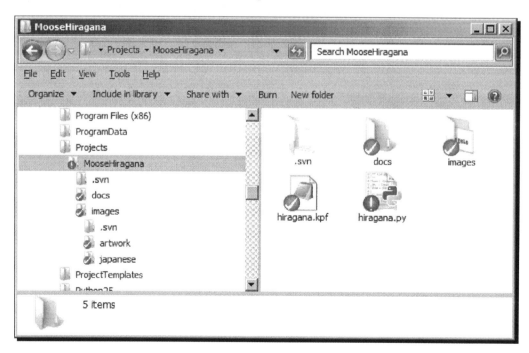

2. Right-click inside the folder and choose **SVN Commit...** (you can also right-click on a specific file, if that is the only file you wish to commit).

3. When the **Commit** dialog box appears, enter a note in the **Message:** text box explaining the changes you have made to the file.

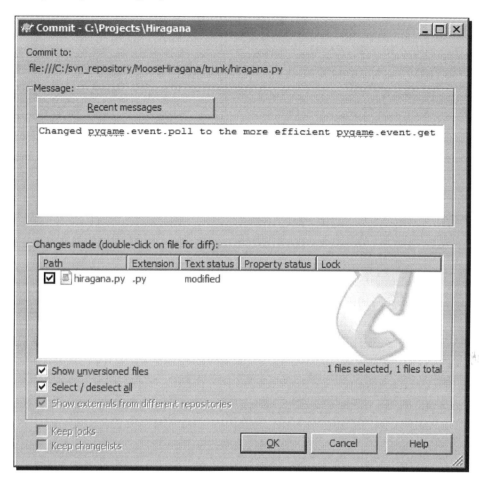

4. Notice that the **Commit** box offers a spell-checking feature. Words that the spellchecker does not recognize are highlighted with a dashed red line under them. The words shown in this example are spelled correctly (**pygame** is the name of a Python library which is used in the application). The spell-check feature works just like the spell-checking feature in Microsoft Word—to see suggestions for alternative spellings, right-click on a highlighted word.

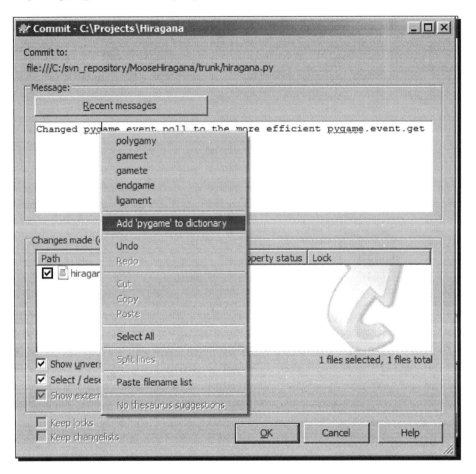

5. Since pygame is spelled correctly, instead of choosing an alternative spelling, click **Add 'pygame' to dictionary**. Pygame will no longer be flagged as being spelled incorrectly.

6. To see the differences between the original file and the modified one, double-click on the filename in the **Changes made** section of the dialog.

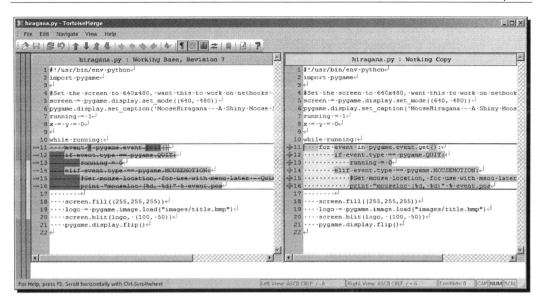

7. Click **OK** to commit the changes.

8. A dialog will appear showing which files have been modified and the status of the commit process.

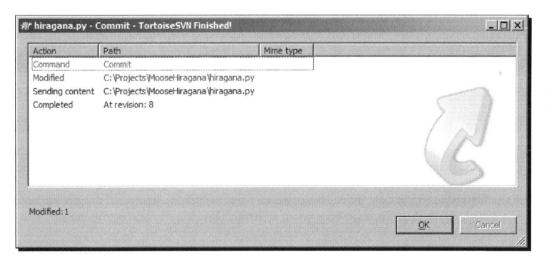

What just happened?

You have successfully changed some files and committed the changes to the repository. Now other developers will be able to download your changes and add to the work that you have done.

You can view differences between text files or images. Images can be viewed in **TortoiseIDiff**, which shows a side-by-side comparison between different versions of a file, and also allows you to layer the different versions for a more detailed comparison:

You may be wondering what would happen if two people both decided to modify the same file at the same time. The good news is that Subversion is equipped to handle such events for most file types.

If the file being edited is a text file or some source code, then Subversion can cope with two or more people editing the same file at the same time. When the users submit their changes, Subversion will allow them to merge their changes into the new version of the file. If the changes cannot be merged for any reason, then Subversion will flag a conflict, alerting you to the problem so that you can resolve it and decide which changes to keep or discard.

To prevent conflicts while you are working on files—be they images, documentation, or source code, it is possible to lock the file that you want to work on, preventing anyone else from committing changes until you release the lock.

Locking files and managing conflicts will be discussed in *Chapter 4*, *Status information and Conflict management*.

The importance of commit log messages

Commit log messages give you a chance to describe the changes that you are committing. It is good practice to provide a descriptive commit log message with each change that you commit—not just to explain to other developers what your changes do, but also to provide a record of the work that you have done.

Commit log messages could be used as the basis for patch notes which will be released to your end users, or could be used by your manager to see how much work you have put into a project. It's likely that your manager will be more impressed with:

```
Fixed "Bug #123 – client crashes when player submits high score" by
correcting the variable name to hiScore (matching naming convention).
```

than they would be with a blank commit, or a message such as following:

```
Change hiscore to hiScore.
```

Of course, you should comment your source code too, but a good commit log message should explain what you changed and why you changed it.

It is possible to add some basic formatting to a commit log message using the following formatting conventions:

Formatting convention	Style
your text	Bold
your text	Underline
^your text^	Italic

In addition to the spell-checking feature already discussed, the commit log message box also supports filename and function auto-completion. The auto-completion box will appear automatically after you have typed the first three characters of the name of a file or a function included in your commit.

You can also bring up the auto-complete box by typing one or two characters from a file or function's name, and then pressing *Control + Space*:

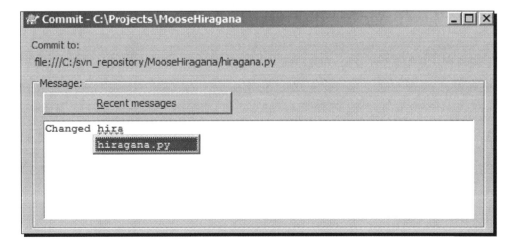

Have a go hero – committing some changes

In the previous *Have a go hero* section you checked out some image files. Change the images, and then commit the changes to the repository. Leave a clear commit log message to explain what you have done.

Excluding items from a commit

There are a couple of reasons why you may want to exclude an item from a commit. The two main reasons are as follows:

- ◆ Your IDE creates files which contain personal settings and data—the content of these files may differ from developer to developer. These files do not need to be synched, so can be excluded from the commit process permanently.

- ◆ Your IDE has changed the timestamp on a project file—but the rest of the file has not changed. There is no need to commit the file every time the timestamp is changed. It makes sense to exclude the file temporarily.

In the first instance, you can set up template files which are subject to version control and contain the basic IDE settings most people like to use for their project. The template file can be renamed to indicate that it is a template, and individual developers can copy the template file and give it the correct file extension.

To ensure that the actual project settings files are excluded from versioning, let's create a rule which tells TortoiseSVN to ignore those files when performing a commit. This can be done by creating a special setting—the `svn:ignore` property for the file in question.

To add a file which is not currently versioned to the ignore list, simply right-click on it and select `TortoiseSVN | Add, to ignore list | File Name`. Or, if you want to ignore all files of that type—for example, all Komodo `.kpf` files, select `TortoiseSVN | Add to ignore list | *.kpf`.

Time for action – excluding files that are already versioned

You may be wondering how to exclude a file from versioning if you have already accidentally committed it. Fortunately, this mistake is easy to rectify.

1. Hold down the *Shift* key and right-click on the file you want to remove from versioning. This will bring up the extended context menu.

2. Select **TortoiseSVN | Delete (Keep Local).**

3. A red X icon should appear on the icon of the file you do not want to be versioned.

4. Now right-click on the file and select **SVN Commit....**

5. Once the commit has completed, right-click on the file and select **TortoiseSVN | Add to Ignore List | filename**

6. You should see the ignored file get a new overlay icon (similar to the following one shown below), indicating that it has been ignored.

What just happened?

You have just removed a file from versioning without removing the local copy. After you removed the file, you committed the changes to the Subversion server, and then told TortoiseSVN to ignore any changes to that file in the future.

This works well for files which change frequently and are not an integral part of the project, but what if you need to submit one or two changes to the server, but are not ready to submit all your changes? In this case, you can choose to temporarily exclude certain files from the check in.

Time for action – temporarily excluding files from committing

1. Imagine that you have been making some changes to **hiragana.py**, and you have also decided to create a small Help feature, which is contained in a file called **help.py**. You are ready to commit your work on the Help feature, so you right-click on the file and select **Add...** to add it to the server, but you are not ready to commit **hiragana.py**.

2. Right-click inside the Working Copy folder and select **SVN Commit...**

3. In the window that appears, ensure that **help.py** is ticked and **hiragana.py** is un-ticked in the **Changes made** list.

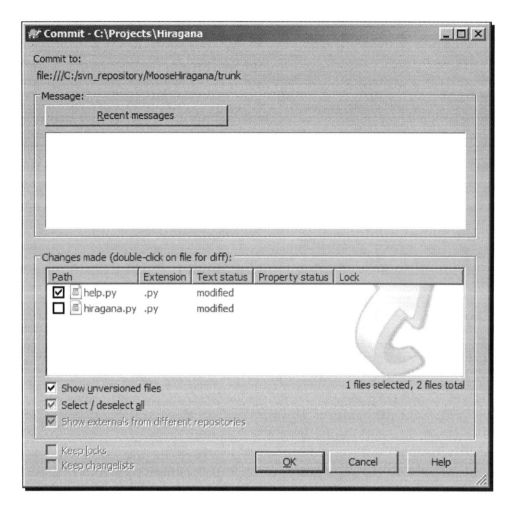

4. Now, when you click **OK**, only the changes to **help.py** will be submitted.

What just happened?

You have successfully submitted the changes you have made to one file without updating other files that you have changed. This is a temporary measure and next time you go to make a commit, the files that you ignored this time will again appear in the commit list. If you want to ignore a certain file on every commit (for example, a file relating to your own IDE settings), then you could move that file to the ignore-on-commit change list, so that you don't have to worry about it in the future.

Committing one file at a time

Instead of right-clicking inside the working directory folder and selecting the files you do not wish to commit, you could simply right-click on the file that you wish to commit, and open a commit dialogue for only that file (or the files that you have selected—if you have selected several files by using the *Shift* or *Control* keys and clicking on the files you want to commit). This can save you a lot of time if you wish to commit only one or two files. This approach should be used sparingly, however, because you run the risk of missing warnings about unversioned files that you would otherwise see if you committed from the root of your working copy folder.

If you want to ensure that a file type is ignored on a long term basis, then you can either use the ignore list detailed in the previous *Time for Action*, or, to ignore a file type across all Subversion projects accessed via this particular client, then you should add the file to the client's Global Ignore list:

Time for action – using the global ignore list

1. Bring up the TortoiseSVN context menu and select **Settings**.

2. In the **General** section of the Settings - TortoiseSVN window which appears, add the file type or filename that you wish to ignore to the end of the list in the **Global ignore patterns** box (patterns are separated with a space):

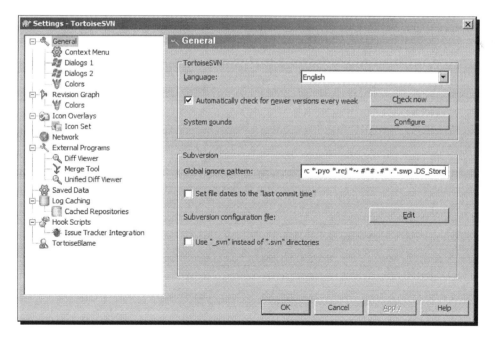

3. Click **OK.**

What just happened?

You have just added a file to the global ignore list—this list is used by the copy of TortoiseSVN on your machine. Any files included in the list will be ignored when you make a commit to any Subversion project. The global ignore list is specific to your client (TortoiseSVN is not the only client that has a global ignore list, other clients use it too, but it is not something that is sent to the server or shared with other members of your team), so other developers using other computers may have different settings and may ignore different files to you.

The ignore list uses Unix-style **wildcards** to match filenames:

- ◆ * : This wildcard matches any string of characters—including empty strings and spaces
- ◆ ? : It matches any single character
- ◆ [...] : This matches any one of the characters contained within the brackets—for example [A-Dprz] would match the upper case characters A, B, C, or D, and the lower case characters p, r, and z

Keeping your working copy up-to-date

You should periodically update your working copy to make sure that you have the latest version of any files that you are working on. This ensures that you are working with the latest version of the source code, and are not wasting your time working on code that has been altered or fixing bugs that have already been fixed.

If you have been following all of the *Have a go hero* sections, your main working copy is most likely out-of-date right now, because your artist has changed some artwork and committed the new art files to the server.

Time for action – updating your working copy

1. To update your entire working copy, right-click inside the folder, and select **SVN Update** (You can update only specific files or folders by selecting them, then right-clicking on them. Developers probably wouldn't want to do this, but it is still a useful feature. An artist working remotely may choose to update only specific assets to save bandwidth.):

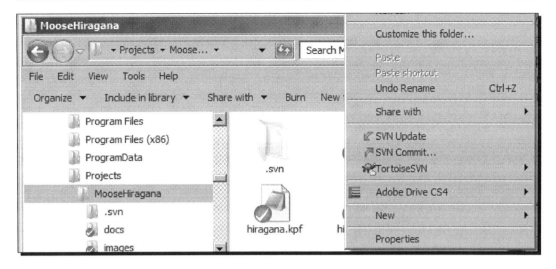

2. An update window will appear, listing files which were added, removed, merged, or updated:

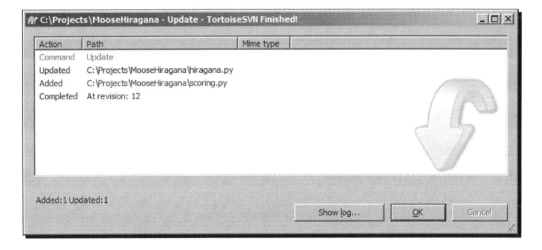

What just happened?

You have just updated your local working copy with any changes that have been made recently and submitted to the Subversion server. This is useful because it allows you to stay up-to-date with the work being done by your colleagues.

Using the repository browser

There may be some cases where you do not want to check out a working copy, but would prefer to perform actions directly on the repository. This is not advisable for routine development work, but can be useful in some instances. The **Repository Browser** allows you to explore a large project's file structure without checking out the entire project's directory structure. It also allows you to view revision logs and blame, and download unversioned copies of files quickly and easily.

The repository browser is intuitive and easy to use.

Time for action – using the repository browser

1. To access the repository browser, simply right-click anywhere in an Explorer window and select **TortoiseSVN | Repo Browser**.

2. The **Repository Browser** window will appear, as shown:

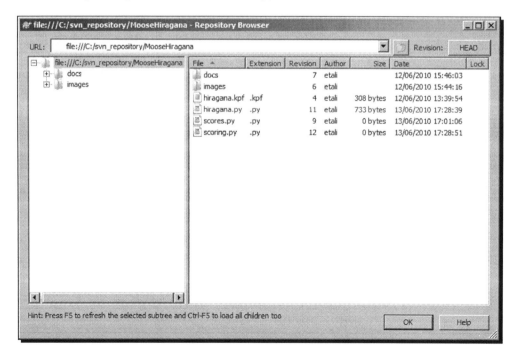

3. The **Repository Browser** works in the same way as Windows Explorer—you can double-click on a folder to expand it. To get more information about a file, right-click on the file you are interested in—you will see several options:

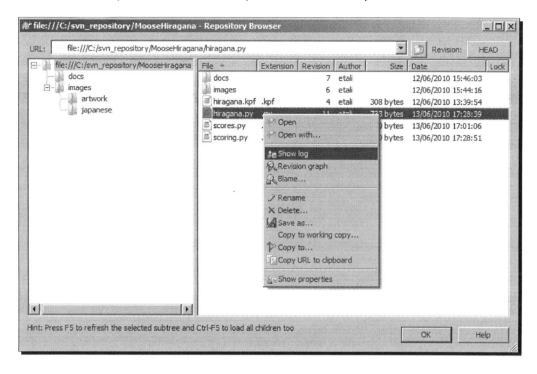

4. The **Open** and **Open with...** options allow you to open the file to view or edit its contents. The **Show log**, **Revision graph**, and **Blame...** options allow you to view information about the changes that have been made to the file.

What just happened?

You have just interacted directly with the repository. Remember that the Repository Browser allows you to work with the files stored on the repository—not your working copy. So, if you delete or rename a file using the Repository Browser, it will be removed from the current version on the repository and therefore be removed from other people's working copies next time they update them.

The Repository Browser is a useful tool for viewing the directory structure of a project and looking at revision histories. However, you should not make a habit of altering files by accessing the Subversion server directly. In most cases, it would be better to make the changes on your local copy, and then check them in.

Pop quiz – working with TortoiseSVN

1. The repository browser is:

   a. A part of Internet Explorer that lets you browse repositories inside your web browser.

   b. Used every time you access a remote repository.

   c. A tool that allows you to interact directly with the repository without checking out a working copy.

2. The global ignore list:

   a. Is a list of files/file types that the Subversion server should ignore. The list is sent to all Subversion clients that access that Subversion project.

   b. Is a list of files/file types that TortoiseSVN should ignore. The list applies to all Subversion projects accessed by that particular client.

   c. Is a feature on the Subversion website that lets you ignore other Subversion users, in case the site is plagued by spammers and trolls.

3. For pattern matching, the global ignore list uses:

   a. Regular expressions.

   b. Unix-style wildcards.

   c. Exact matches only.

Summary

In this chapter, you used TortoiseSVN to perform some of the more common day-to-day version control tasks—checking out a working copy, making changes, and checking those changes in.

Specifically, we covered:

- Checking out a working copy
- Using the `checkout depth` feature to check out only the parts of the repository that you need to work on
- Checking in your changes
- Excluding items from a commit

We also touched base on some of TortoiseSVN's other features, including file locking, commit log messages, and the repository browser.

This chapter covered the ideal scenarios. In the real world of software development, things will not always be this simple. In *Chapter 3, Creating and Applying Patches*, you will learn about patching—how to create and apply patches, how to track revisions using the Blame feature, and how to work with revision graphs.

3

Creating and Applying Patches

This chapter deals with patching—one of the most important parts of software development. Patches are incredibly useful for open source projects because they allow people to submit small changes to a software project without needing write access to the repository. TortoiseSVN makes it easy to create and apply patches, as well as keep track of who has made which changes.

In this chapter we shall:

- ◆ Learn what patching is for
- ◆ Learn how to create and apply a patch
- ◆ Learn how to track changes with Blame
- ◆ Learn about tracking contribution statistics

So let's get started...

Why use patching?

Shiny Moose Software is a fairly small software house. All of the developers have write access to the repository. This is fine because the developers know and trust each other. They know that their colleagues will not deliberately damage the repository, and if they were to make a mistake and commit some bad code, Subversion will save the day by making it possible to revert to an older, working version.

This particular access model doesn't scale very well, however. So, when Shiny Moose Software decided to make the basic version of Moose Hiragana open source, it became obvious that they needed some other way of handling permissions.

The two most obvious options—allowing everyone to write to the repository, or requiring that people fill out some kind of application form before getting access, wouldn't work very well. Giving everyone, including complete strangers, write access to your repository is simply asking for trouble. But making people pass some form of application test will deter new contributors—very few people would bother take the time to fill out a form and apply for access to a repository if the application process took longer than fixing the bug itself.

The solution to this problem is to use patches. Most open source projects use patches to filter contributions from new developers. Instead of giving everyone the ability to commit their changes straight to the repository, unknown developers are given the chance to submit a **patch** file. This patch is reviewed by one of the core developers, who can reject the patch, ask the patch author for some changes, or accept the patch and submit it to the repository.

Anyone can submit a patch. All they have to do is download the code, make the change that they want to submit, and then use TortoiseSVN to create a patch.

What is a patch?

A patch is a simple text file which shows the differences between the original files and the modified working copy. The patch file tells Subversion what to do to integrate the changes with the copy on the repository.

Once the patch has been created and submitted, a developer with rights to commit code to the repository can check the patch and ensure that it meets the project's standards. Typically, an acceptable patch must fix something that is generally agreed to be a bug. The patch must follow the project's coding standards (for example, variables must be named according to an agreed standard), and the patch must not introduce any new problems into the code.

A flow chart showing a patch review process from an average open source project is shown as follows:

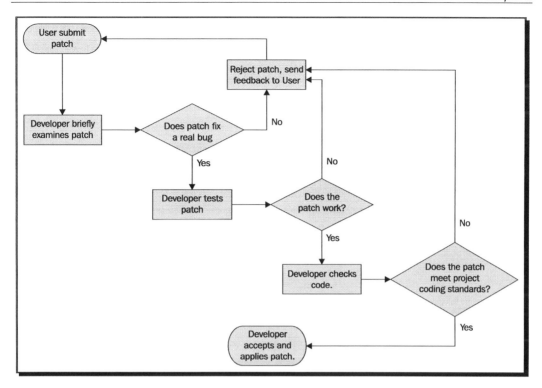

Does the patch fix a real bug?

The previous question may seem like a strange one—aren't all bugs real? Well, sometimes users can view a design decision as a bug if it produces behavior that they see as undesirable. For example, when the Maximize, Minimize, and Close buttons were re-ordered in the Lucid Lynx release of Ubuntu (a popular GNU/Linux based operating system), there was a lot of debate about the change, and lots of bugs were filed (`http://bugs.launchpad.net/ ubuntu/+source/light-themes/+bug/532633`). Canonical had made a deliberate decision to make the change, but there was a vocal group of users and volunteer developers who were unhappy with it. If every patch that was submitted got accepted then the developers would end up playing a game of User Interface ping pong, racing to submit changes to get the buttons where they felt they should be. Reviewing patches ensures that volunteers patch only things which are accepted as bugs.

How to create a patch

Let's imagine that a user, called Tineladia, has found a simple bug in MooseHiragana. Tineladia has noticed that one of the roll-over menus on the options screen does not change when the mouse cursor is moved over it. Tineladia happens to be a developer and knows that the bug is simple to fix, so they decided to create a patch and submit it to Tiny Moose Software.

Time for action – creating a patch

1. Check out a working copy of the source code for the project that you want to patch.

2. Make the required change to the code.

3. Test the change to make sure that the modified code runs correctly.

4. Right-click in the working copy folder, and select **TortoiseSVN... | Create patch...**

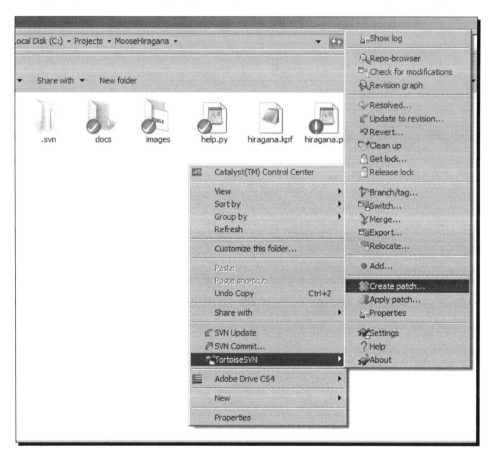

5. The **Create Patch** window will appear. Ensure that there is a tick in the box next to the file (or files) which you have changed, and click **OK**.

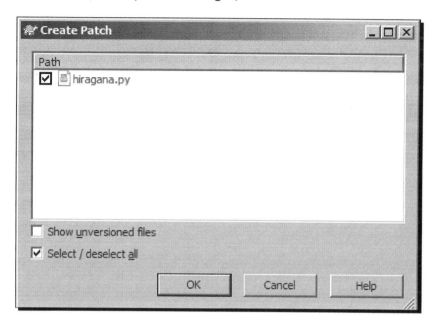

6. When prompted for a file name, give the patch a descriptive name. If you are submitting a patch that solves a bug report listed on a bug tracker, you may want to include the bug number in the patch. Shiny Moose Software does not currently have a bug tracker, so Tineladia chose a simple but descriptive file name, menu_bug.patch.

7. After saving the patch, **TortoiseUDiff** will appear. This window shows the differences between the base source and the working copy the patch was built from. Select **File | Exit** to close the window.

```
menu_bug.patch - TortoiseUDiff                                    _ □ X
File
1 Index: hiragana.py
2 ===============================================================
3 --- hiragana.py (revision 22)
4 +++ hiragana.py (working copy)
5 @@ -16,7 +16,7 @@
6
7  startBut2 = pygame.image.load("artwork/start2.gif")
8  optionsBut2 = pygame.image.load("artwork/options2.gif")
9 -scoreBut2 = pygame.image.load("artwork/scores1.gif")
10 +scoreBut2 = pygame.image.load("artwork/scores2.gif")
11  exitBut2 = pygame.image.load("artwork/exit2.gif")
12
13  screen.fill((255,255,255))
14
```

What just happened?

You have just created your first patch using TortoiseSVN. A patch is a simple text file that contains some information about the directory it was created from, and a list of the differences between the base copy and the working copy it was created from.

As well as creating a patch from a folder, you can create a patch based on a specific file. This is useful if you have changed more than one file in the folder, but are submitting just one specific patch at this time.

Now that you have created the file, you can submit it to the developer of the software. Most open source projects have a bug tracker which you can use to submit patches. We will talk about bug trackers in more depth in *Chapter 9, Using TortoiseSVN with Bug Tracking Systems*.

Tiny Moose Software does not have a bug tracking system set up at the moment, so Tineladia chose to e-mail the patch to the developers. When Quinn opens the e-mail, he can examine the patch, test it, and then—if it is good enough—apply it.

Copying the patch to clipboard

You can copy the patch into your clipboard from within TortoiseUDiff. For a short, simple patch, this can be useful for sending details of your code changes to a mailing list for review. It is common for attachments to be forbidden on busy mailing lists.

Applying a patch

Quinn has tested Tineladia's patch, and decided that it meets all of the criteria required for a patch to be applied—it fixed a genuine problem in a non-controversial way, it does not introduce any other problems, and it works well.

Quinn decides that the patch should be incorporated into the code for the next version. So now it is time to apply the patch.

Time for action – applying a patch

1. Open the patch, and look at the first line to determine where the patch was created from.

2. Copy the patch file to the correct folder in your working copy.

3. Right-click the patch file and select **Apply patch...**

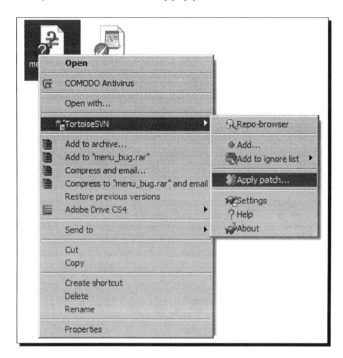

4. Double-click the name of the file in the left-hand window which appears.

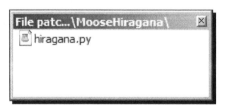

5. A **TortoiseMerge** window will appear showing you the difference between the original and the patched file.

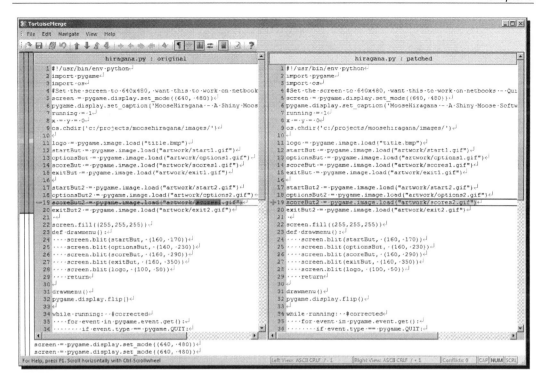

6. If you are happy with the changes, save them.

7. From here, you can check on your working copy, make more changes yourself, or apply other patches, then check on all the changes in one go.

What just happened?

You have just applied a patch. The method described in the previous *Time for Action* is just one way of applying a patch. You can also apply patches without copying them to the working copy directory. If you right-click inside the working copy directory and select **TortoiseSVN | Apply patch...** when there is no patch file present, TortoiseMerge will prompt you to select a Diff file.

If you attempt to apply a patch by right-clicking on the patch file when that file is not located inside the correct working copy directory, TortoiseMerge will prompt you to select the correct working copy folder, as shown in the following screenshot:

Determining the folder level a patch was made from

The first line of the patch indicates the path to the file that was modified. Imagine that the full path to the file being modified was /docs/languages/ en_uk.po

If the first line of the patch file said: Index: docs/languages/en_uk.po

It is clear that the patch was created from the root of the project. If the path in the first line was instead languages/en_uk.po, then the patch was created from within the languages folder.

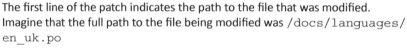

Have a go hero – more on patching

As mentioned earlier, patches need to be applied to the same directory as the one they were created from. If you attempt to apply a patch to a different directory, TortoiseSVN will tell you that you are using the wrong directory, and attempt to suggest the correct one.

Experiment with creating patches at different levels within the project, then applying them to other levels to see how the first line is altered to reflect the path of the file modified, and to see how TortoiseSVN responds.

You'll quickly find your own preferred method of applying patches, but perhaps the easiest way is to right-click and drag the patch file (the source file) over the destination file to apply the patch. When you release the mouse button you will be given an option to Apply Patch.

Tracking changes with Blame

If your project has a lot of contributing developers, it may become difficult to keep track of the changes being made to the code. An easy way to see who has changed each line of code is to use TortoiseSVN's **Blame** feature.

The term **Blame** sounds rather negative, but really the feature can be used for positive reasons. For example, you could use the Blame feature to see which developers have been the most productive in terms of the number of lines changed. In fact, in some localized versions of TortoiseSVN, the terms "annotate" or "praise" are used instead of "blame".

The Blame feature allows you to see who has changed a specific line of code, and why. This means that if you find a line of code that looks strange, you can look at the last person who changed it, and read any commit messages they left to see if there's a reason for the line to look the way it does. You can then make a much more educated decision as to whether to change that line of code (if you think it is the cause of a problem or bug), or leave it as it is and consider other routes to solving your problem.

The Blame feature is also useful for due diligence. It can be used to keep track of which contributors changed the code. In some open source projects, some files are released under different licenses to others. If a license is ever violated, the project will be able to identify who changed the offending code, and inform them of the problem.

Time for action – using Blame to track changes

1. To view **Blame...** for a file, right-click it and select **TortoiseSVN | Blame...**

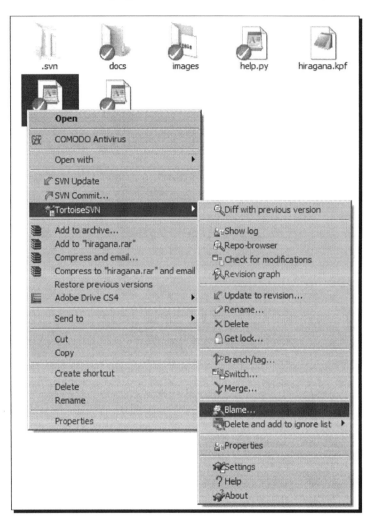

2. The default settings will show the Blame history for all revisions to the file, ignoring line endings and whitespace. To view only recent changes, change the **From revision** number to reflect the revision you want to start tracking Blame from.

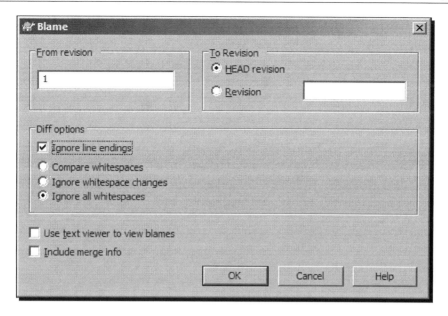

3. The **TortoiseBlame** window will appear, showing who is responsible for the current state of each line of code in the file:

What just happened?

You have just viewed the blame information for a file within your project.

In the previous example shown, there are two contributors whose code is currently included in the project file. The user with the name Etali has had the most impact on the current status of the file, however another user, with the user name Moose, has added some comments and altered some lines.

The screenshot shows the Blame screen as it would appear with TortoiseSVN's default settings. That means that pink lines are lines which have recently been modified, while pale blue lines are lines which have not been altered recently. The colors can be changed by going to **TortoiseSVN | Settings...** then opening the **TortoiseBlame** section:

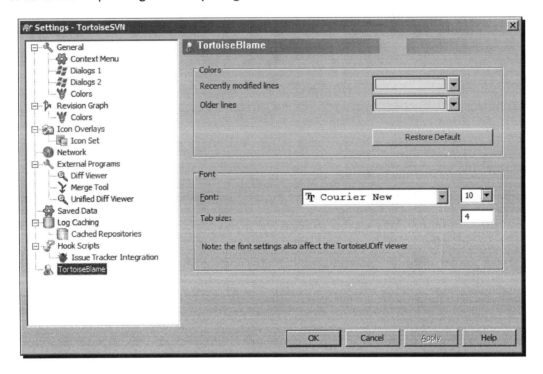

For more granular Blame information, you can also view blame for specific revisions via the log:

Time for action – using the log

1. Inside your working copy folder, select **Tortoise SVN | Show Log...**

2. The log messages window will appear. Right-click on the revision you are interested in, and select **Compare and blame with previous revision**.

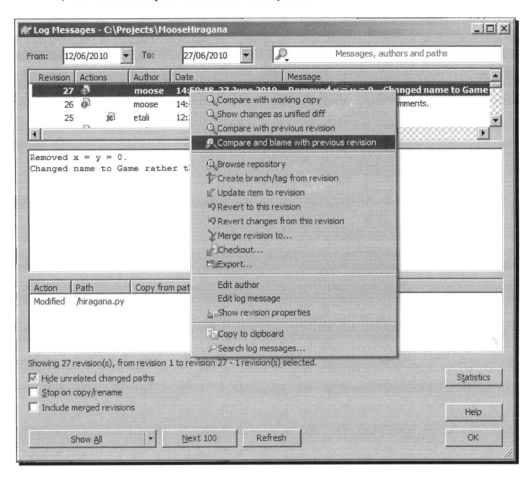

3. The **Changed Files** window will show a list of files which were modified in that revision. Right-click on the file you are interested in and click **Blame revisions**.

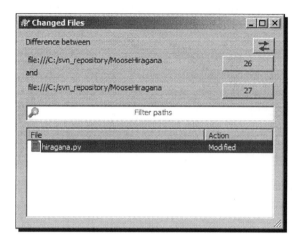

4. The next window will show the lines which were changed, indicate who created the line in the previous revision, name the person responsible for modifying it in this revision, and give the date and time of the change.

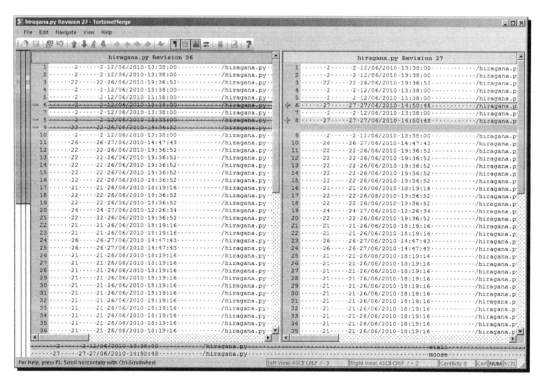

5. If you have a small monitor, you may find that the revision window looks rather messy—you can use the horizontal scrollbars to scroll past the revision number, date, and time information to see the actual lines of code which were changed, or, if you prefer, you can hold down the *CTRL* key while using the scroll wheel to scroll the screen horizontally.

What just happened?

You have just tried another way of viewing Blame information. This method is useful if you are viewing Blame and revisions for a large project. So far, the examples we have explored with Shiny Moose Software involve only a couple of developers working on a small number of files.

Tracking blame for individual files is fairly easy no matter how you do it, but when the project gets bigger, being able to see the revision history at-a-glance using the TortoiseSVN Log feature will make life a lot easier.

As well as allowing you to view Blame information, the log gives you an easy way to view commit log messages. **Commit log** messages often contain information about the reason for a change (for example, Added verification on user input - Fixes Bug #1234). If you are ever unsure as to why the latest commit changes something in the code you are working on, the first place you should look (after the comments in the code itself!) is the commit log messages.

Working with statistics

Blame offers an easy way to see who is responsible for the current code in particular files within a project, but what if you want an overview of the whole project?

TortoiseSVN makes it easy to see statistics for the number of developers working on your project, and the number of commits they have made. You can see this data in raw numeric form, or in chart form.

This information can be useful as a way of seeing which developers are the most active, and of tracking their efficiency. While it's not always true that the volume of code someone is producing is an indicator of how good a developer they are, you can use number of commits as one form of measuring how much work is getting done. This information could help you determine whether developer sprints or crunches are helping or hindering your team's development efforts.

Time for action – viewing statistics

1. Open the TortoiseSVN Log window, as you did in the previous *Time for Action*.

2. Click the **Statistics** button. The **Statistics** window will appear.

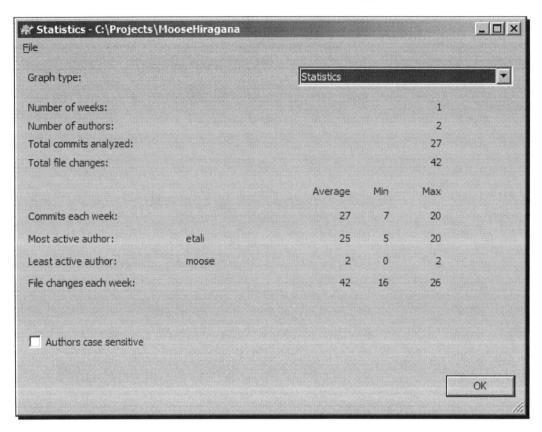

3. The first page shows some raw data relating to the number of authors, the number of commits, and the number of files which have been changed.

4. To view the information in graph form, select the graph you want to see (**Commits by date** or **Commits by author**) from the **Graph type** menu.

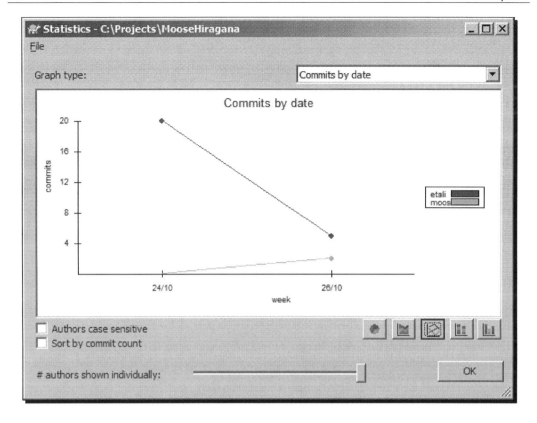

5. You can change the graph used by clicking one of the buttons across the bottom of the graph. The options are: Pie graph, Stacked line graph, Line graph, Stacked bar graph, and Bar graph respectively.

6. If your project has a lot of people working on it, you may find it helpful to use the **# authors shown individually** slider to specify how many authors to display on the graph.

What just happened?

You have just viewed the statistics for your current project. The statistics give you a long term view, or a week-by-week view, of the number of commits made on a per-author basis. You can see raw data or a range of different charts depending on your preferences.

This information is useful to help you track the most active contributors, and can help you to see what percentage of commits are coming from which developers. You can see who your most active contributors are, and see if there are more or fewer commits being made on a week-to-week basis. The list shows the most recent 100 entries. If you need to see more than that, then you can fetch the rest of the entries by clicking the **Get All** button.

Pop quiz – working with TortoiseSVN

1. Patch files are useful because:

    a. They allow people without write access to the repository to submit source code changes to your projects.

    b. They hide the source code from people who are not developers.

    c. They are the only way to fix bugs.

2. A patch file is:

    a. A unified diff file that shows the change between the base copy and the working copy.

    b. A binary file that contains instructions that only Subversion can understand.

    c. A modified copy of the original file, containing all the lines—both those that have been changed, and those that are unchanged.

3. Blame is used to:

    a. Track who changed each line of the source code.

    b. Assign or remove points from people, depending on how many bugs they introduce.

    c. Highlight which developers are good, and which are (b)lame.

Summary

In this chapter you used TortoiseSVN to create a patch file and to apply a patch. You also learned how to track changes with Blame, and how to work with revision graphs. Specifically, we covered:

◆ Patches—why use them, and how to create and apply them.

◆ Tracking changes with Blame

◆ Using the statistics page to get information about contributor activity

◆ How patches are used in a real world open source project

We also discussed differences. A patch file is simply a file which shows the differences between the base copy, and your modified working copy.

Now that you are familiar with patching, it's time to learn about file statuses and conflicts. It is inevitable that you will encounter some conflicts during your software development career, and *Chapter 4, Status Information and Conflicts*, will equip you to deal with them.

4

Status Information and Conflict Management

*So far you have learned how to create a working copy, submit changes (or a patch), and synchronize those changes with the server. The examples you have seen were all quite simplistic—one person makes a change and checks it in, and then another person checks out an updated copy and makes their own changes. In the real world, things are rarely that simple. What if two people try to make changes at the same time? This chapter will explain the different **statuses** that files can have, and talk about file conflicts and how to resolve them.*

In this chapter we will:

- ◆ Learn about the different file statuses and what they mean
- ◆ Learn about file **locking**, and what it can be used for
- ◆ The different kinds of conflicts you are likely to encounter
- ◆ Learn about **tree conflicts** and file conflicts and how to resolve them

So let's get started...

File statuses

TortoiseSVN makes it easy for developers to see, at-a-glance, the current status of the files in their working directory. If you've been following the examples in the book so far, you've probably already seen some of the file status icons in Windows Explorer—for example, the icons for Normal and Modified. These icons are added as an overlay icon on top of each file in your working directory.

There are nine statuses in total, and the statuses can apply to files or directories.

The following table shows the file statuses, and the icons used to represent them:

Icon	Status Name	Meaning
	Normal	This is the status you want to see. A freshly checked out working copy (which matches the contents of the copy on the Subversion server) will have this status.
	Modified	The modified status applies if you have made a change to that file or directory.
	Added	When a file is scheduled to be added to version control (but has not yet been added), this status applies.
	Locked	This file status indicates that you hold a lock on a file. Locks will be discussed in depth later in this chapter.
	Ignored	This file status indicates that, for the purposes of version control, this file or folder is being ignored.
	Read Only	This file status indicates that the svn:needs-lock property has been set on this file. The file will be read only until you can get a lock on it.
	Deleted	This status indicates that the file is scheduled to be deleted from version control, or that a file under version control is missing from the folder.
	Conflicted	This status indicates that a conflict has occurred. Conflicts will be discussed in depth later in this chapter.
	Non-versioned	This status indicates that the file or folder has been excluded from version control

Your icons may look slightly different.

The icons shown in the previous table are just examples. If you are using the default settings for TortoiseSVN, the status overlays (the ? symbol, crosses and exclamation marks, for example) will look the same as the ones shown previously. The underlying icon may differ depending on the IDE or application associated with the file that you are working with. The files shown in the preceding table were associated with a range of applications—including WordPad, Notepad, and Komodo Edit.

File locking

File locking is a feature of Subversion which can be used to optionally "lock" a file that you are working on so that others cannot commit changes to it. This feature is not usually used for source code because changes to source code files can usually be merged fairly easily. File locking becomes useful when you are working with files that are not trivially mergeable.

Shiny Moose Software started as a fairly small team, and originally used the dreaded "programmer art" (placeholder graphics created by a developer rather than an artist) while working on their MooseHiragana application. Now that the application is almost finished, Quinn has decided that the graphics created by Mowbray aren't good enough, so they've hired an artist, Mariah, to create some better graphics.

Mariah checks out the images directory to take a look at the images created by Mowbray. While she's working on re-creating the images, Mowbray notices that he has made a mistake. The image file for the character "Wo" contains the graphic for the Hiragana character "Ya", and vice-versa. He corrects those two images and commits his changes to the repository.

Mariah, not being well versed in the ways of source control, spends the day making attractive versions of every single character in the Hiragana alphabet, and then decides to commit them all at once. Mariah does not realize that Mowbray has changed two of the files, and when she tries to commit those files, a conflict arises.

Fortunately, in this case, the files are small and simple, so it won't take long for Mariah to check out the updated files and make the required changes, but in the real world that will not always be the case.

File locking is a way to prevent such problems from occurring. In general, it is not advisable to lock text files or source code, but it is a good idea to lock images, video files, audio files, and other files that are not trivially mergeable.

Mariah now needs to update the game's logo. She decides to lock the file before working on it, to avoid a re-run of her previous problems. She also decides to help her fellow artists out by setting the `svn:needs-lock` property of the image files so that others are warned that the file should be locked before they work on it.

Time for action – setting the needs-lock property

1. Using Explorer, choose the file that you would like to set the `needs-lock` property for. If you want to set needs-lock for multiple files, hold down the *CTRL* key while clicking each file to select them.

2. Right-click on the files and go to **TortoiseSVN | Properties**.

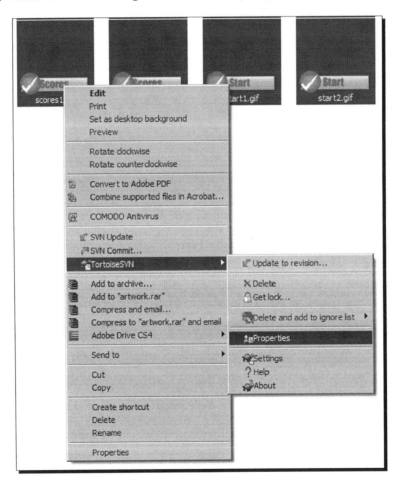

3. The Properties dialog will appear. Click **New...**

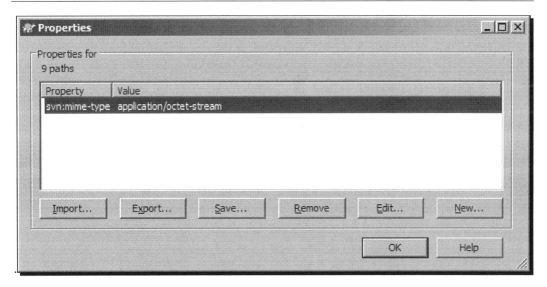

4. Select **svn:needs-lock** from the **Property name:** dropdown, and enter a suitable message in the **Property value:** box, then click **OK**.

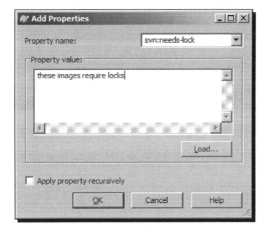

5. The files that you set the lock for will now have the **Modified** status. Commit your changes.

6. If you attempt to modify one of the files which requires a lock, you will be warned either upon opening the file, or when you attempt to save it, depending on the application you are using. The following screenshot demonstrates the warning message that you will receive. The following screenshot demonstrates the warning message that you will receive:

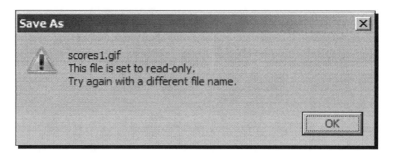

What just happened?

You have just set the `svn:needs-lock` property for some image files.

If a file is set to require a lock, then it will be checked out as read-only if the person checking out the file does not obtain a lock on the file. Many applications warn users when they try to open a read only file for editing. Some applications, however, will not display any messages about the status of the file until the user attempts to save it.

Whether you choose to require file locking for certain file types within your project is a decision that you will need to make yourself, based on the policies of your team. Some teams work well with file locking, but smaller teams may prefer to rely on other methods to co-ordinate their work on files that are not easy to merge.

Once the needs-lock property has been set for a file, anyone who wishes to edit that file will need to obtain a lock on it before they are permitted to edit the file. This does not mean that only files that have the `needs-lock` property set can be locked. It is possible to lock any file. However, files that have the `needs-lock` property set **MUST** be locked before they can be edited.

Time for action – locking a file

1. Update your working copy (right-click on the file or folder and select **SVN Update**) to ensure that you have an up-to-date copy of the file you want to work on.

2. Next, right-click on the file and select **TortoiseSVN | Get Lock...**:

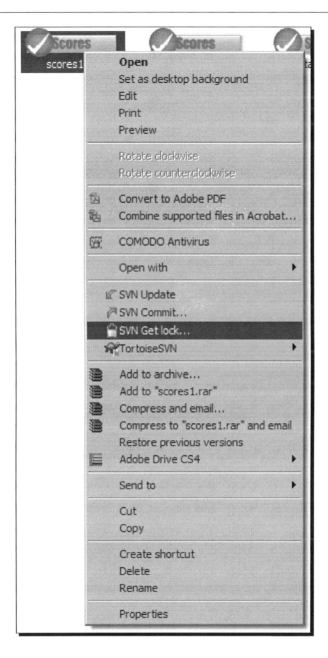

3. The **Lock Files** dialog will appear. Enter a message describing why you are locking the file(s) so that your team members will know what you are working on.

What just happened?

You have just locked a file. When you have a lock on a file, other people who attempt to work on the file will be warned that you have a lock on it.

In Subversion, locks are optional, and intended as a communication tool, rather than a core part of Subversion's version control features. You should not rely on locking for security or control of a file. Locking is a simple mechanism which is there as an extra layer of protection. It is not intended to replace good team communication, and should not be used as such!

Getting a lock on a file that has needs-lock set

If a file has needs-lock set, then TortoiseSVN makes it even easier to obtain a lock. Instead of having to look for the option on a submenu, TortoiseSVN will show the **Get Lock...** option at the top level of the right-click menu, saving you precious time!

Stealing a lock

Mariah requests a lock on the splash screen for MooseHiragana. She starts working on the file, but it takes longer than she expected to complete the work. She goes home for the day, planning to finish the work the following day. Unfortunately, Mariah falls ill, and has to take some extended time off work. She hasn't released the lock, so what happens if someone needs to work on the file while Mariah is recovering from her illness?

The good news is that it's possible to **steal a lock** from another user, so if someone accidentally locks a file and forgets to release the lock, you aren't stuck in a position where the file isn't easy to edit.

Locking is a communication aid, not security

Locking is designed to be used as a communication aid. A way to tell your team mates "Please don't touch this, I'm working on it!". It is not designed as a security tool. Don't lock a file and then assume that nobody will touch it while it is locked, and then leave it locked for a long period of time. If you aren't working on a file, release the lock. If you don't want the file to be locked, then protect it some other way. Don't rely on locking!

Time for action – stealing a lock

1. Select the file that is currently locked, right-click it and select **Get lock...**.

2. Enter a message for your colleagues, explaining the reason for the lock, and tick the box that says Steal the locks.

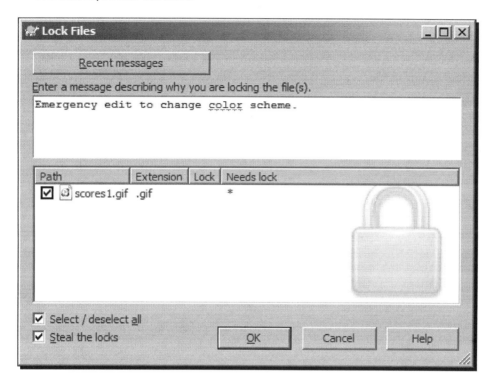

3. The dialog that appears will indicate that you now have a lock on the desired file.

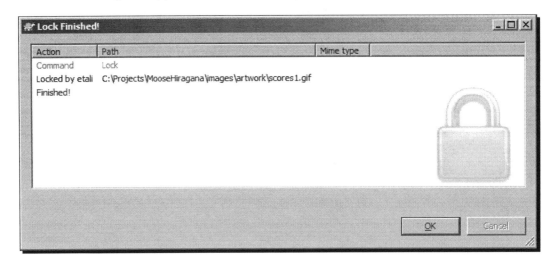

What just happened?

You have just stolen a lock. This command is a powerful one, and should be used responsibly. In general, you should avoid stealing locks unless all other possible routes for resolving the lock problem have failed.

If a staff member locks a file, then leaves the office and is un-contactable, then that may be a good reason to steal a lock so that you can correct an urgent problem.

In contrast, you probably shouldn't steal a lock on a large and complex 3D image that a designer is working on so that you can correct a small problem—especially if the designer has been working on boning the model all day, and you know that they're just away from the keyboard to grab some lunch! Your minor change can wait until the artist gets back to their desk.

Stealing a lock is not a substitute for good communication!

Remember that after you steal the lock and commit your changes, you should release the lock. It's possible that the user you stole the lock from may then commit their changes, overwriting the work that you have done. Your colleague will be warned of a conflict if they try to do this, and they should use the conflict resolution tool to find out what has happened, but it is possible that they could decide to overwrite your changes.

It is important to remember that locks are assigned to a specific working copy, rather than to a specific user. This means that if you, as a developer, get a lock on a file while you are using your main workstation, you will not be able to edit that file on your laptop computer. It is the working copy that owns the lock, not the user.

Don't forget to release your lock once you have finished making changes to the file in question.

Releasing a lock is a simple process:

Time for action – releasing a lock

1. To release a lock, right-click on the locked file and go to **TortoiseSVN | Release lock**:

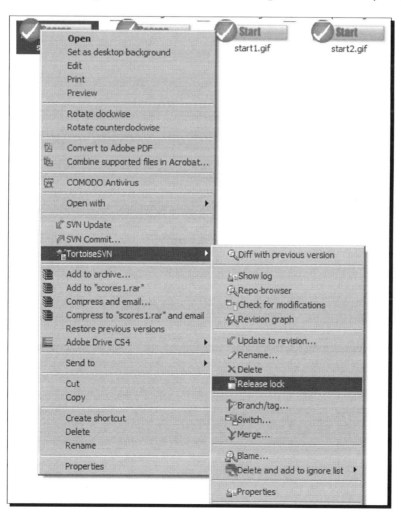

2. The **Unlock** dialog will appear. If you had selected more than one file to release locks on, then all the files will be listed here. Un-tick any files you don't want to release the lock on (in this case, only one file is being unlocked, so no changes are required) and then click **OK**.

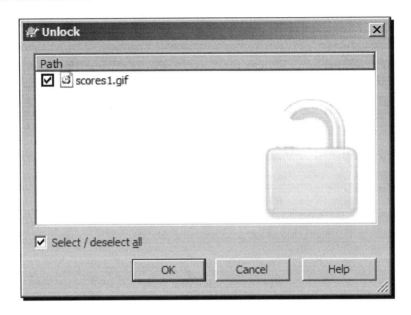

What just happened?

You have just released a lock that you held on a file. Now that the file is no longer locked, other users are free to work on it and make changes as they wish.

> **Releasing locks via folders**
>
> It's also possible to release a lock on a file (or multiple files) by right-clicking on the folder that the files are part of, and selecting Release Lock. You will be greeted with a list of the files within that folder that you currently have a lock on.

If you commit a file, then by default the lock you have on that file will be released during the commit process. This means that the only time you should need to release a lock manually is if you decide that, for some reason, you do not wish to commit any changes that you have made.

Resolving conflicts

Locking a file is designed to prevent conflicts—if only one person is working on a file, then nothing unexpected can happen.

However, file locking isn't used every time someone wants to work on a file. It doesn't make sense to restrict editing of source code or plain text files in cases where most edits are on unrelated areas of a file, and are unlikely to conflict with each other.

That said, sometimes conflicts do happen, and when they do, you need to be able to resolve them.

This chapter will describe the three main types of file conflict. Conflicts can also arise with branches, and this subject will be discussed in *Chapter 5*, *Branching and Merging*.

The most common file conflict is:

♦ Local edit/incoming edit

While the most common tree conflicts are:

♦ Local edit, incoming delete on update

♦ Local delete, incoming edit on update

♦ Local delete, incoming delete on update

Scenario 1 – local edit, incoming edit

This kind of file conflict occurs quite frequently if two users try to edit the same part of the same file at once.

Let's imagine that Quinn and Mowbray both perform a check out, and then start working on the same file, the `Questions.py` file. Quinn sees that Question 3 doesn't follow the conventions used for the other questions, so he changes the question completely and then commits the new question file with the re-worded question. Mowbray spots the same problem, but instead of completely changing the question, he re-words the question to make it read the same way as the other questions in the game. While he is working on that, he also standardizes some capitalization in the files—ensuring that all characters are written in the same case throughout. He then attempts to commit his changes.

When Mowbray attempts to make his commit, he will be warned that there is a conflict. SVN will create a file conflict, inserting conflict markers into the question file, and creating a `.rej` file for the files that are in conflict.

At this point, Mowbray has three choices. He could:

1. **Scrap his own changes, and accept the changes that Quinn made**: This is the easiest option. All he has to do is revert his own changes and update his working copy.

2. **Keep his own changes, ignoring the changes Quinn made**: This will update the `Questions.py` file so that it matches what Mowbray has done, destroying any changes that Quinn made to the file.

3. **Manually merge the changes**: This requires some manual editing of the file which is in conflict. In the previous example, Mowbray may decide that Quinn's modification of Question 3 is a good idea, and decide to use it, but that the work that he did on standardizing the case of the Romaji versions of the characters is too important to lose. So he would merge those changes into one file, and then commit that file.

Exactly how you handle this kind of conflict in your own software project is up to you. Option A is the easiest and fastest way to handle a conflict, but that does not mean it is the best way. Your colleagues probably won't be impressed if you always trash their own changes without giving a second thought to the work that they have put in!

If you decide to go with Option C, then you should update your working copy to make sure you have the most up-to-date version of all the files you are working on. Fix any other minor conflicts you may encounter, merge the changes that you think need merging, and then commit the new file.

File locking can prevent this kind of conflict from occurring, however, it's important not to over-use file locking. If you think that it's likely that someone else will attempt to edit the same part of the file that you are working on, or that the file you are working on is not trivially mergeable, then it is a good idea to use file locking—but be aware that if you lock a file, then you are preventing other people from modifying it, so don't hold on to locks for too long. You will achieve nothing but irritating your colleagues if you do!

Scenario 2 – local edit, incoming delete

Quinn has decided that MooseHiragana is going to cover more than just Hiragana. He wants to add a second level to the game which will teach Katakana—the alphabet that the Japanese use to write words which are not from their own language.

To facilitate this change, Quinn decides to tidy up the project's file structure. He decides that instead of storing the flash-card files for both alphabets in `/images/japanese`, the project should use a different folder for each alphabet.

He moves all of the Hiragana flash-cards to /images/japanese/hiragana, and creates a second folder, /images/japanese/katakana for the Katakana flash cards. He then commits his changes to the repository.

While Quinn was making this change, Mariah noticed that the graphic to represent the Hiragana character 'Sa' was incorrect. She edits the character and saves her changes. When she commits the changes to the repository, she is informed that there is a conflict—Sa.bmp no longer exists in the /images/Japanese folder, so Mariah needs to decide what she should do.

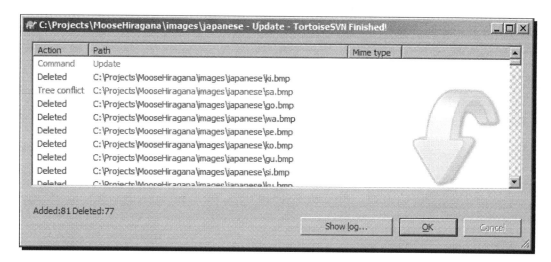

In this case, Mariah could revert Quinn's changes (Which would be a bad idea in this case), or she could find out where Sa.bmp has been moved to, and move her version of the file to the correct place, then commit her changes.

Before Mariah can make a decision about what to do with her files, she clicks **Show log...** to find out why the conflict has occurred. Quinn may not have bothered to send a memo round the office, or actually speak to his artists to tell them about the structure change, but he has left a fairly helpful note in the commit logs. Mariah sees the note, and now understands that all she has to do is move her updated graphic into the new /images/Japanese/hiragana folder and then commit her changes.

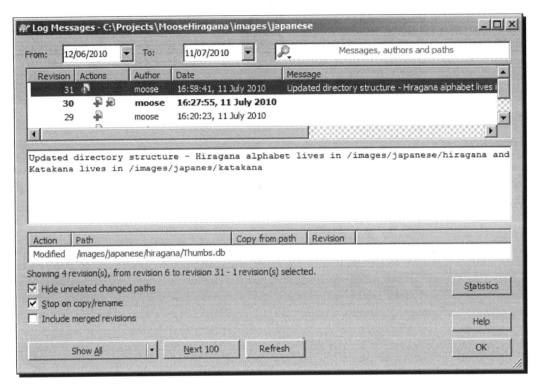

Mariah can then mark the conflict as resolved by right-clicking on the conflicted folder and selecting **TortoiseSVN | Resolved....** This will bring up the **Resolve** dialog box. Mariah just has to make sure that the files which are no longer in conflict are selected, and click **OK**. From then on, Updates and Commits can continue as normal.

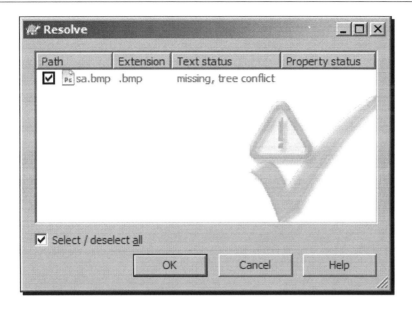

Scenario 3 – local delete, incoming edit

While Mariah has been working on MooseHiragana's graphics, Mowbray has been focusing on the client-server code, so that people can submit their high scores to a leaderboard and play competitive games. Mowbray created two servers using different network libraries and ran some performance tests before deciding which library to use.

When Quinn saw the results of the performance tests, he quickly decided that the server library used in the file `server2.py` was better than `server1.py`. He deletes `server1.py`, and renames `server2.py` to `server.py`. He then commits his changes.

While Quinn was doing this, Mowbray spotted a bug in his server code. He quickly fixes the bug, and committed his changes. A conflict arises because Quinn is trying to tell Subversion to delete a file that has an incoming edit.

As described in the previous example, Quinn has the choice of discarding his update (effectively deciding not to delete the file), or discarding Mowbray's edits by marking the conflict as resolved without doing anything.

If Quinn is lucky, the **Conflict Edit** dialog will offer to merge the incoming edit into the re-named version of the file, however depending on where the Commit was run from, TortoiseSVN may not be able to identify the new name of the file.

Scenario 4 – local delete, incoming delete

Quinn and Mowbray are both working on the multiplayer code for MooseHiragana. They both decide that `chatc.py` is not an acceptable file name for the chat client. Quinn renames the client to `chatClient.py`, following the naming conventions which were decided upon at the most recent developer meeting.

Mowbray didn't attend the meeting, so he does not know about the new standards. He renames the file to `client.py`.

Quinn commits his changes and leaves a commit log message explaining the new naming convention. Now, when Mowbray commits his changes, three things will happen:

1. `Chatc.py` is marked as deleted and has a tree conflict.

2. `chatClient.py` is added to his working copy, with a status of 'normal'.

3. `Client.py` is marked as added with history.

If Mowbray wants to resolve this conflict, he will have to find out what the new name for `chatc.py` was in the repository. He can find this out by reading the comments posted by Quinn in the commit log.

After manually resolving the conflict, Mowbray should mark the conflict as resolved—either using the conflict editor or the right-click menu option in Explorer.

Pop quiz – working with TortoiseSVN

1. File statuses tell you:

   a. The size of the file.

   b. The type of IDE that the file was written in.

   c. The current status of your Working Copy version of the file compared to the file on the server.

2. Which of the following would create a conflict:

   a. Incoming deletion of `main.py`, outgoing edit of `server.py`

   b. Incoming deletion of `main.py` (renamed to client.py), outgoing deletion of `server.py` (renamed to `network.py`)

   c. Incoming edit of `main.py`, outgoing deletion of `main.py`

3. Locking should be used:

   a. Files should be locked every night before you go home.

   b. On any file that you happen to be editing, to stop others from editing it.

   c. On files which are not trivially merge-able, such as audio, video, or complex document formats.

Summary

In this chapter you learned the meaning of the different file statuses used by TortoiseSVN. You also learned about the conflicts that can occur when several people work on the same file on a Subversion server, and you learned how to deal with those conflicts.

Specifically, we covered:

- The meaning of the different file statuses
- When and how to use file locking
- The different kinds of tree conflict
- How to resolve conflicts

The examples in this chapter were incredibly simplistic, and are not suggestions for how a real software house should be run. In fact, working at Shiny Moose Software sounds like an incredibly stressful job! In the real world, one would hope that a software project would be planned out from the start, and that refactoring on such a huge scale would not happen on a regular basis. In fact, the project should be planned out well enough that the project's overall file structure should not change often (or at all) during development. Feature creep in the form of adding entire new game modes should not happen either.

The conflict examples given in this chapter are simply used as a way to describe a problem that could arise, and how the problem could be fixed. As always, being organized from the start and communicating well with your team is a much better way of coping with occasional changes and conflicts.

That's not to say that the information in this chapter is unimportant. Even in a large software house where there are agreed standards and layouts for almost every purpose, there will be occasions when you will encounter conflicts.

Good communication within your team can help to reduce the number of issues that you encounter. How you manage that communication is up to you. With larger teams, communicating through mailing lists or team meetings is impractical. In that case, clear comments in your code and concise, clear commit log notes can work wonders for keeping people informed and ensuring that all members of your team get the information they need, at the time that they need it.

In the next chapter, you will learn about branching and merging, and managing conflicts within branches.

5
Branching and merging

*So far you have learned how to create a working copy, submit changes (or a patch), synchronize those changes with the server, and handle some of the simpler conflicts that may arise. The examples you have seen all involved one development project. In the real world, there are a number of reasons why a team may want to run more than one development branch at a time. This chapter will explain **branching** and **merging**, and also cover some of the common conflicts that can occur when you are working with development branches.*

In this chapter we shall:

- Learn why branches are useful
- Learn how to create a branch, and how to switch your working copy
- Learn how to merge a branch back into the **trunk**
- Learn how to merge one or more branches
- Learn about TortoiseSVN's new merge tracking features
- Learn about the conflicts that can occur when merging a branch, and how to deal with them.

So let's get started...

What is a branch?

Branching is an important, but often overlooked, part of source control. Branching allows you to maintain more than one version of your software at once. The main version—which will be worked on by the majority of your developers—is called the **trunk**. The other versions are called **Branches**.

Branches allow your team to test "what if" scenarios, work on large code changes, or make separate versions of your software, without affecting the trunk. This is useful because it allows the main development process to continue in the background—while those large changes are being made on a separate development branch of the software, small bug fixes and updates can be done on the Trunk, and released to your customers after testing so that they don't have to wait a long time for essential updates.

What is a tag?

Another useful feature in a similar vein to branching is **tagging**. This feature allows you to mark a specific revision so that you can easily recreate it on demand. Tagging is often used to mark release versions.

In the eyes of Subversion, tags and branches are the same thing—a directory that contains a snapshot of the project. What separates a tag from a branch is the way that we, the users of Subversion, interact with the tag. As long as nobody ever makes a commit to a tag, it remains a tag. If your team starts committing to a tag directory, it becomes a branch. It's possible to configure a Subversion server to prevent people from committing to a tag directory, but not all systems administrators choose to do this. If you don't have a paranoid systems administrator, then you can still use tags. If someone mistakenly commits to your tag directory then you can undo their changes easily enough!

Why use branching?

There are many reasons why you may want to use branches. Usually, branches are employed to separate code changes from the main project—either to prevent problems, or to allow the project to "branch off" in two or more separate directions.

One reason to use branches would be to allow easy development of a multi-platform project—one branch for Windows, and one for Linux, with the common files being kept in the trunk. Another reason could be to allow bug fixes and minor updates of an already released software version to continue, while other developers work on a major overhaul of the software for a new version.

Not all software projects use branching. Some projects, especially comparatively small ones, may find branching to be overkill, and instead of relying on branches, have check-in rules that ensure the stability of the code. For example, you may be told that you should not check in any code unless it does not adversely affect the functionality of the current version. So, you could check in a partially implemented feature—as long as that code does not break anything that worked in the previous version.

If you're working on a project with rules similar to those previously mentioned, then you aren't completely losing out on version control features. Tagging, for example, can be used—you can check out a specific revision number to see how the code looked back then.

Common branch types

A few of the more common scenarios are listed in the following section. This list is not exhaustive. In the following diagrams, a solid arrow represents a branch, while a dotted arrow represents a merge.

Branching on new releases

With this branching system, each new release becomes a branch. Common changes—for example, essential bug fixes or security updates, are merged between releases. When an older release is no longer supported, the branch for that release is killed off.

Release branches are created rarely—perhaps one or two a year. They are maintained for long periods of time, only being killed off when a specific version of the software in question is no longer supported. Security patches and other important changes may be merged into several different branches, but other updates—cosmetic changes or new features, are likely to be added only to the most recent branch.

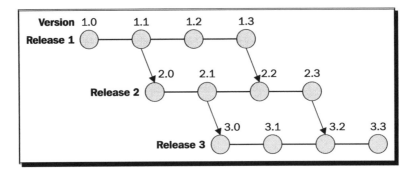

Branching on promotion

This method of branching creates a new branch for every tier. When changes have been tested fully they are promoted and merged into the next tier, and the branch relating to that change is killed off:

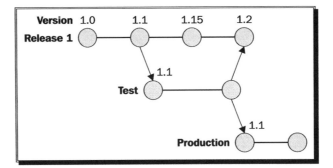

Branching per task

This branching strategy treats every development task as a new branch. Once the task has been completed and tested, the code for that task is merged back into the trunk and that branch is killed off.

This branching strategy is favored by some teams because it fosters a low-risk environment— changes are made in their own branches, so the risk of a thoughtless commit causing problems for other developers is low. However, excessive branching can make collaboration difficult, and can create a lot of extra overheads.

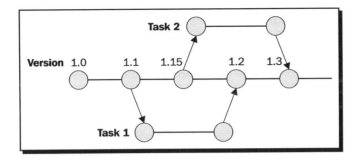

Branching components

This development strategy involves running a branch for each architectural component of the software being developed. When a component is completed, it is merged back into the trunk. The branch life cycle looks a lot like the cycle shown in the preceding diagram for Branching per task.

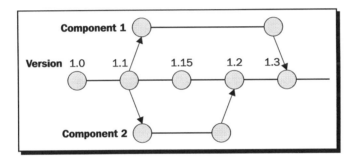

A branch for each platform

This is a common branching strategy for multi-platform projects. With this branching strategy, the core (or **Common**) code is kept in the trunk, while platform specific code (for example, Linux, Windows, or Mac specific code) is handled in branches.

In this development strategy, the branches will live for as long as that platform is being supported.

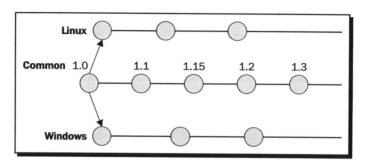

The good news for Shiny Moose Software is that Python and PyGame, which the MooseHiragana game is built upon, are designed from the ground up to be portable. There's little need to run separate branches for Windows and Linux. Some other languages and frameworks are not as portable, so it's still good to be aware of the option of branching for the platform specific parts of your application.

Common branching pitfalls

Branching is a useful way to separate different code streams, which can be useful to ensure the stability of your project. Requiring people to carefully merge their changes will act as a buffer to prevent people from accidentally breaking the entire project with a dodgy commit.

That said, branching has its own problems. Some of the things you need to watch out for are:

- **Merge fear**: Some developers may want to avoid merging because they are worried that it will go wrong. You should take measures to stop this attitude promptly—monolithic merges are more likely to be dangerous than more frequent, bite-size ones.

- **Excessive merging**: If people are spending more time merging than they are writing code, then there's something wrong.

- **Excessive branching**: If you need a map almost as complex as an A-Z of the world to track your branches, it's probably time to reconsider your development practices.

- **A permanent temporary branch**: This oxymoron is all too common. If your temporary branch has been around for the lifespan of the project, maybe it's time that its purpose gets defined?

Branches are for the minority

When correctly used, branches are for the minority. Most of your development work should be taking place in the trunk. If you find that your team is spending more time on a branch than they are in the trunk, there's a good chance that your development strategy needs examining. There are exceptions, but in general, spending most of your time on branches is a sign of problems somewhere in your development strategy.

Creating a branch

If you have a well organized directory structure, then creating a branch or a tag should be a simple matter.

The following is an example of the directory structure that could be used for the MooseHiragana project:

- `/repositories/MooseHiragana/trunk`: This contains the main code.
- `/repositories/MooseHiragana/branches`: This folder could then itself contain:
    - `/windows`
    - `linux`
- `/repositories/MooseHiragana/tags`: This contains
    - `/Release-1.0`
    - `/Release-1.1`

This directory structure is optional. The important thing is that the directory structure you choose is one that works for you and your team, and is clear, consistent, and easy for new team members to follow.

If you hadn't been planning on using branches, you may have chosen to keep your working copy in the root folder of your project. This works OK if you are always working on the trunk and making trivial commits, however things can quickly get confusing when you add branches. For this reason, it's a good idea to observe a directory structure similar to the previous one in your repository.

Branches and tags don't use a lot of drive space

Subversion doesn't use the traditional method to create a branch or a tag. Instead, Subversion achieves the same result using a cheap copy, which is somewhat similar to a **hard link** in Unix. This has a pleasant side effect in that the drive space usage of a Subversion branch is lower than what you might expect. If you aren't familiar with the idea of hard links, think of them as a sophisticated version of a shortcut in Windows.

At Shiny Moose Software, Quinn decides that it would be a good idea to have a branch for the development of the Katakana version of Moose Hiragana. This will allow the language specialists to work on the logos, flash cards, and scoring system for the Katakana version of the game without interfering with the development of the Hiragana version.

Time for action – creating a branch

1. Right-click inside your working copy and select **TortoiseSVN | Branch/Tag**.

2. Enter the Subversion URL that you want the branch to have. In this case, we remove/trunk from the URL and change it to `/branches/moosekatakana`:

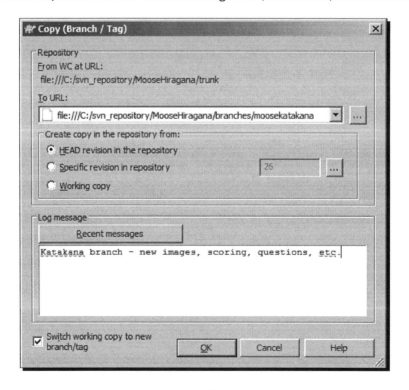

3. Select **HEAD revision in the repository**, assuming you would like to create the branch based upon the most recent revision. If you would like to create a branch based upon a different revision, or your current working copy, then you can do so by selecting the relevant option in this window. You can enter a revision number manually, or select a revision from the window that appears when you click the **...** button.

4. Tick the checkbox that says **Switch working copy to new branch/tag**.

5. Your working copy will be switched to the branch that you have just created, and you will see a dialog box confirming what changes have been made:

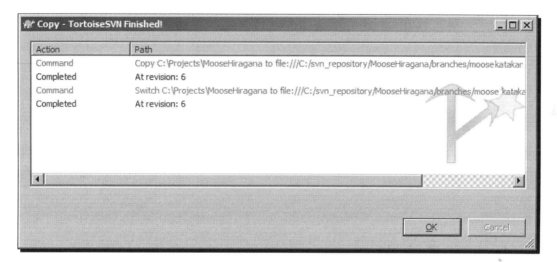

What just happened?

You have just created a branch and switched to it. Now, when you work on this working copy, any changes you commit will be sent to the branch, not the trunk. The target URL is shown at the top of the commit dialog, so you can easily tell where you are committing to (the trunk, or a branch).

In the future, other branches could be created for other versions of the game, for example, a Kanji version, or a version for learning German, that teaches words, rather than letters of the alphabet.

This isn't the most ideal example of a use of branching—it would be much better if Shiny Moose Software's flashcard game had been designed to be modular from the ground up that would make changing the purpose of the software as simple as swapping out the images and the list of questions. Unfortunately, Quinn did not plan for flexibility, so there are many things which are hard coded into the application that should really be handled in a more modular way.

Deadlines are looming and Quinn cannot afford to start rewriting MooseHiragana at the moment, so for now, branching saves the day. A more wise use of branching would be to create a branch which can be used to extensively refactor MooseHiragana to allow new flashcard packs to be easily imported. While this development work is going on, other team members can spend their time working on new language packs for the Kanji version of the original game. This keeps existing customers happy, while still allowing the team to work on a neater and more efficient code base for future versions of the game.

Tagging and selecting revisions

You can create a tag in the same way that you created a branch. Instead of changing the path to `/branches/nameofbranch`, set the new path to `/tags/Version-Number`.

When creating a branch, you chose to use the **HEAD revision in the repository**. When creating a tag, you may want to use a different version of the code. You can do this by selecting a specific revision in the repository, then entering the revision number. This is useful if you released your project a few days ago, but didn't make a tag at the time. If there have been several commits since then, and you can't remember exactly what revision number you need, click the **...** button to bring up the revision log and select the correct revision from there. Tags created in this way require no data transfer from your local working copy, and are therefore created quickly.

A shortcut for creating a branch or tag from a revision

Another way to create a branch or tag from a revision is to use the log dialog. While inside the log dialog, right-click on the desired revision and select **Create branch/tag from this revision**.

You can also create a tag based upon your own working copy. Unlike the other two options, this form of tag creation is quite complex—your working copy will need to be synchronized with the repository, and this may take some time depending on the number of changes that have been made.

Tagging is useful because it allows you to quickly roll back to a specific revision—usually a major release. This means that if something goes wrong and a lot of files are damaged or deleted—either by accident, or thanks to a malicious staff member or volunteer, a known good copy can be retrieved easily.

Switching your working copy

You have already seen one way to switch your working copy—while creating a new branch; however there will be times when you want to swap between branches or back to the trunk. TortoiseSVN makes it easy to switch between branches.

Time for action – switching your working copy

1. Right-click on the working copy folder, and select **TortoiseSVN | Switch....**

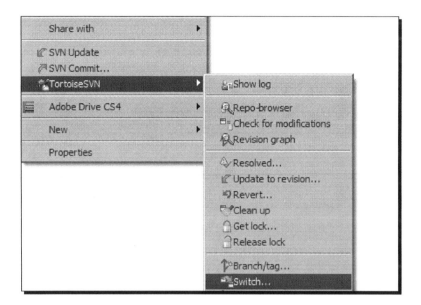

2. The **Switch To Branch / Tag** window will appear. Select the branch or tag that you would like to switch to from the **To URL:** dropdown list, or enter the correct path manually:

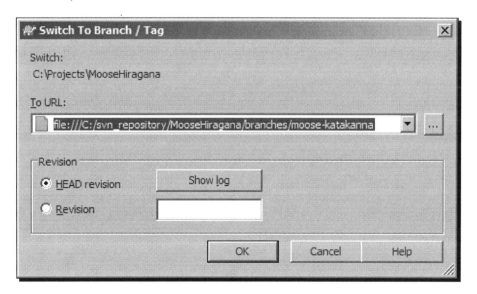

What just happened?

You have just switched your working copy. In the previous example, we switched from the trunk to a branch. You can switch from branch to branch, from a branch to the trunk, or vice-versa.

Switching your working copy is not the same as performing a checkout. A checkout downloads everything from the desired branch (or the trunk) to your working directory. A switch will only transfer the data that has changed. This means that switching creates less stress on the server, and is much quicker too.

Performing a switch will not discard any local changes, they will be merged when you switch. If you do not want them to be merged, you should either revert your working copy to an already committed revision before you perform the switch or commit your changes first.

Reverting changes

In the world of software development, things don't always go right. Sometimes you may find yourself in a situation where you wish you could wind back time. Unfortunately, you can't reverse time in real life, but you can ask Subversion to revert changes for you—giving you a snapshot of how your files looked at last commit (or even several commits before that).

Time for action – reverting changes in your working copy

1. To revert a change in your working copy, right-click in the folder that contains files you want to revert to an older version, and select **TortoiseSVN | Revert** (right-clicking on just one file will select that file as the only one to be reverted).

2. In the dialog that appears, select the files that you want to revert, and then click **OK**.

3. Click **OK**, and a quick revert will be performed, taking you back to the previous version of the file(s) in question.

What just happened?

You have just reverted a file (or some files) in your working copy to their previous version.

But what happens if you want to revert more changes—going back one or more revisions, and making an older revision the new **HEAD revision**? Well, you can do that using the revision log.

Time for action – reverting more changes

1. Select the folder (or file) for which you want to revert the changes.

2. Select **TortoiseSVN | Show Log** to bring up the list of revisions. If you want to go back a long way, you may need to click **ShowAll** to see a full list of revisions.

3. Select the revision that you want to revert. If you want to revert lots of revisions, select the first one, then, while holding down *Shift*, select the last one.

4. To revert back to a much older version, right-click on the selected revisions and select **Revert changes from these revisions**:

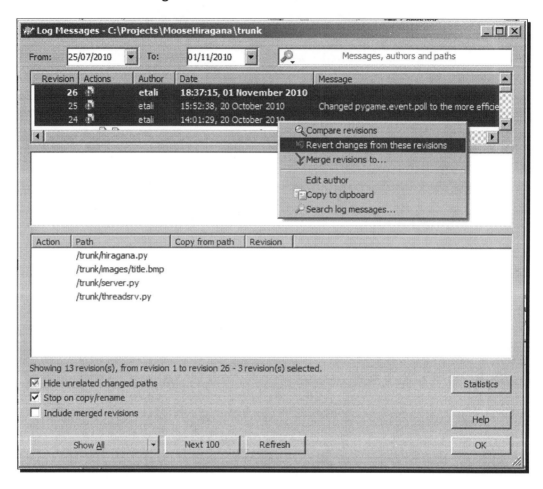

Your working copy will now have been reverted to the revision that you specified.

5. Alternatively, to make a much older revision in the new **HEAD revision**, select that revision, right-click on it, and select **Revert to this revision**:

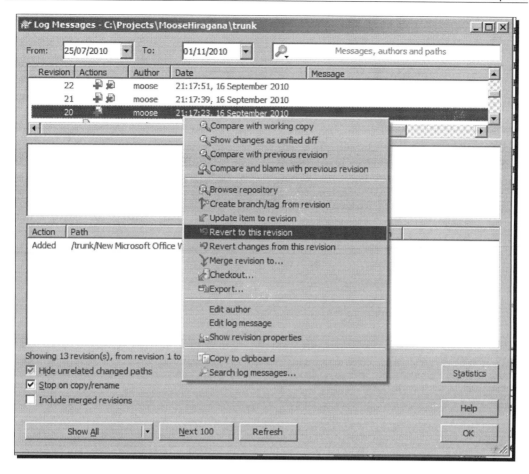

What just happened?

You have just reverted back to a much older revision—effectively rewinding time to get a snapshot of how your project looked at some point in the past.

Merging

Branches contain separate lines of development, but that does not mean that they are destined to go their own way forever. Branches are still linked to the trunk (hence why they are called branches, not, for example, islands). You can merge changes made on a branch to the trunk, or merge changes to the trunk into the branch.

Merging can be a complex process, but there are things that you can do to ensure that the process goes as smoothly as possible:

◆ Always perform merges into a clean working copy—that is, one that does not have any outstanding changes needing to be committed

◆ If you have made changes to your working copy, commit them before merging

◆ After completing the merge, review the results to make sure that the merge went as expected

◆ If the merge didn't go as expected, revert the changes

Usually, when you merge a branch, you will have made several changes to the branch in the course of completing the task that the branch was designed for. This means that you will need to merge all of your revisions back into the trunk.

Merging a range of revisions is the most common action for most projects. Merging a whole branch is something you're likely to do after you have finished working on some changes in a private branch, and you're ready for them to be put into the trunk. In this example, we're merging from a branch, into the trunk.

Time for action – merging one branch

1. Right-click inside your working copy and select **TortoiseSVN | Merge**.

2. The merge dialog will appear. Select **Reintegrate a branch**.

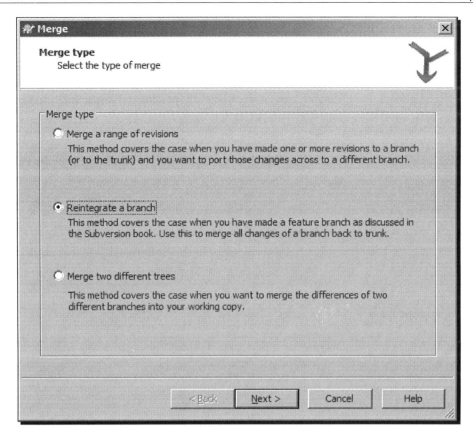

3. Click **Next**.

4. The **Merge** dialog will appear. Select the correct **From URL** if it has not defaulted to the right URL. If for some reason you don't want to merge all revisions, go back to the window shown in Step 2, select **Merge a range of revisions**, and then click **OK**. As shown in the following screenshot, click **Show log** to view a list of revisions:

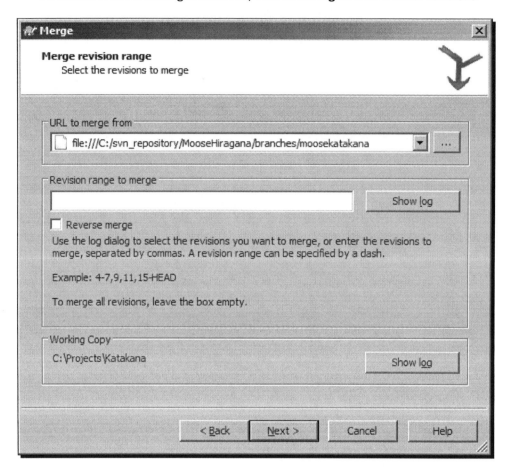

5. You can then select the revisions you want to merge, or make a note of their numbers, and enter the range in the **Revision range to merge** box on the **Merge** screen manually. In most cases, however, you will likely want to merge up to the latest revision, so you should leave the box empty:

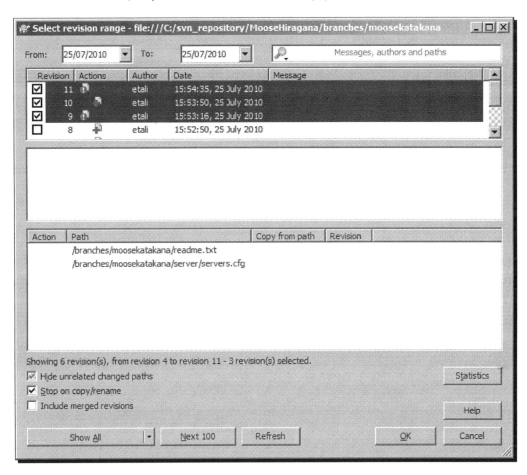

6. Click **Next**. The default options on the following screen are acceptable for this scenario. You can alter the **Merge depth** if required (this follows the same rules as **Copy Depth**, which was discussed earlier):

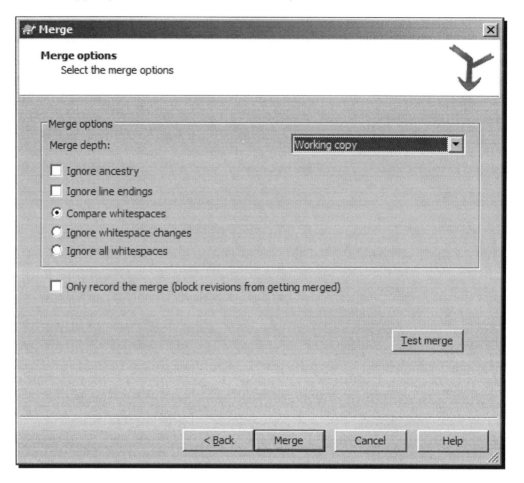

7. In most cases, the default options are acceptable. However, if you are using a programming language that does not care about whitespace, then selecting the options to ignore whitespace and line endings may help to avoid file conflicts. You should not select this option if you use a whitespace aware language such as Python.

8. Clicking **Test merge** will allow you to see if there are any conflicts without actually performing the merge. In this case, **Test merge** shows no problems:

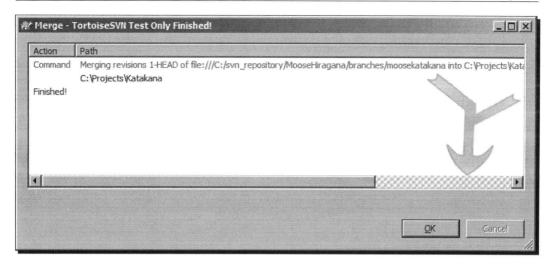

9. Since the test merge went smoothly, we know it's OK to do the merge for real, so go ahead and click **Merge**.

10. Congratulations, you've performed your first merge!

What just happened?

You have just merged some revisions from a branch into the trunk. The revisions being merged in this case were trivial, so there were no conflicts. In the real world, it's likely that there would have been many more complex changes to both the branch and the trunk. You will learn how to cope with the conflicts that can arise in those situations in the following section, *Resolving conflicts on merging*.

Before that, let's look at another common scenario—merging two trees. This method can also be used to merge a branch back to the trunk. This type of merge is designed for special cases (such as a feature branch), where a branch has been regularly synchronized with the trunk, making the branch and the trunk identical except for your specific branch changes, and you need to compare the branch and the trunk to perform the merge.

Whitespace as a language!

This doesn't relate specifically to TortoiseSVN, but if you're interested in the wonder of whitespace characters, then take a look at Whitespace—the programming language. Yes, it's an entire language based on spaces, tabs, and new line characters! The language was created by some students of Durham University who feel that those poor whitespace characters are an overlooked part of computing: `http://compsoc.dur.ac.uk/whitespace/index.php`

Time for action – merging two trees

1. Open the merge wizard from within a working copy of the branch which you want to start the merge.

2. Select **Merge two different trees**.

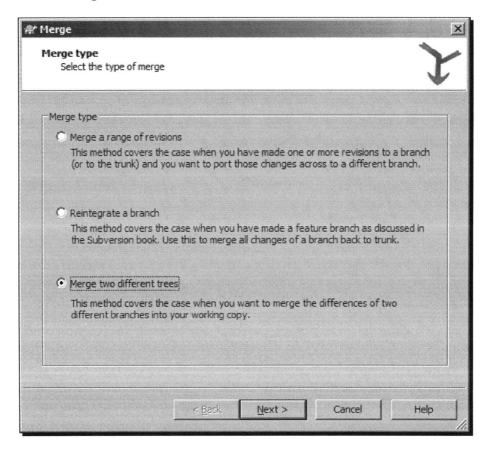

3. In the **From (start URL and revision of the range to merge):** field, enter the URL of the starting branch (or trunk if you are merging back to trunk).

4. In the **To (end URL and revision of the range to merge):** field, enter the URL of the feature branch.

5. If you are sure nobody else will be making commits at this time, you can use **HEAD** in both revision fields. If others are working on the branches in question, specify the revision number you want to use. Don't forget that you can use **Show Log** to find out what happened at each revision:

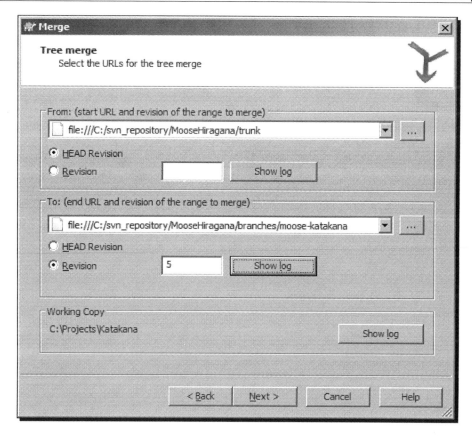

6. Once again, the default options on the final Merge options screen are acceptable in this case.

7. Click **Test merge** to make sure there are no conflicts, and if all goes well, click merge.

What just happened?

You have just merged two different branches, or merged a branch back to trunk, depending on the two paths that you entered.

Merging works by comparing the differences between the two branches, and applying the required changes to your working copy. Your working copy should be clean before you attempt to perform a merge.

The two merges we have done so far in this chapter have gone smoothly, but that won't always be the case. This brings us to our next topic—resolving tree conflicts.

Check the results after each merge

Make sure you check the merge results to make sure that your merge went as expected. It's better to check early than to discover something went wrong later, after several other changes have been committed.

Undoing changes with reverse differences

One use of merging which is often overlooked is to roll back a change that has already been committed. This is useful if you are working on some code and you realize that a major change you made earlier has had some unexpected and undesirable effects. Instead of having to rewrite the code manually, you can do a reverse difference to restore your old, working code.

You may think that this sounds similar to performing a revert, and in a way it is—however, reverts are done on uncommitted changes, and cannot be undone. A reverse merge is done on changes that have been committed to the repository, and can be undone if required.

Resolving conflicts on merging

Merging is a complex process, and the further the branch gets away from the trunk, the more likely it is that there will be problems when you attempt a merge.

The most common conflicts that you will encounter when merging are:

- Local missing, incoming edit on merge
- Local edit, incoming missing on merge
- Local delete, incoming delete on merge

If this list sounds familiar, that's because it's very similar to the conflicts described in the previous chapter, except instead of being caused by updating a file, they come from merging a branch back into the trunk.

Many of the following problems can be reduced in severity (if not completely avoided) by performing frequent merges to make sure that your trunk and branch do not get too far out of synch. If your team members make several changes before merging, then they may end up in a situation where they find it hard to remember the purpose of each change, making it much harder to resolve conflicts. Of course, different teams have different policies, but there is a lot to be said for taking an **Iterative** and **Incremental** approach to development!

Scenario 1 – Local missing, incoming edit

Quinn has been working on the scoring system, and modifies `hiscore.py` in the trunk, then commits his changes to the repository.

Mowbray, while working on the branch, renames `hiscore.py` to `scoring.py` and commits it to the repository.

Merging Quinn's trunk changes to the branch causes a tree conflict. `scoring.py` is in the working copy with a status of 'normal', while `hiscore.py` will be marked as missing with a tree conflict.

Mowbray can fix this conflict either by marking `hiscore.py` as resolved in the conflict editor, and leaving it at that, or by merging Quinn's changes from `hiscore.py` into the `scoring.py` and then marking the conflict as resolved.

Scenario 2 – Local edit, incoming missing

In this scenario, Quinn is working on the trunk and renames `login.py` to `client.py`, and commits his change to the repository.

Mowbray has been adding some extra features to the login feature in a branch, and saves `login.py`. It then commits it to the repository.

When it's time to merge, these changes cause a tree conflict. `client.py` is marked as added, and `login.py` is marked as modified, with a tree conflict.

Mowbray now needs to decide what they want to do. Should they respect Quinn's new naming choices and merge their changes into `client.py`, or just revert Quinn's changes and keep the local file?

With a fairly small project it's easy enough to tell at-a-glance what the new file name should be, but in a project with hundreds of files Quinn may find it useful to refer to the log to find out what's going on. Once Quinn has made the right changes, they can use the conflict editor to mark the conflict as resolved.

Scenario 3 – Local delete, incoming delete

In this scenario, Quinn is working on the trunk and has renamed `login.py` to `client.py` and commits this change to the repository.

Mowbray is working on a branch and renames `login.py` to `authenticate.py`, and then commits this change to the repository.

A merge of Quinn's trunk changes to Mowbray's branch working copy causes a tree conflict. In this case, `authenticate.py` is marked as normal, `client.py` is marked as added with history, and `login.py` is marked as missing, with a tree conflict.

Mowbray must find out what Quinn renamed `login.py` to before they can resolve the conflict. This can be done using the log dialog for the merge source. Once they know what `login.py` is now called on the trunk, they can make a decision as to whether they should respect Quinn's naming choices. After the conflict has been resolved manually, Mowbray must mark the conflict as resolved using the conflict editor dialog.

Tracking merges

In Subversion 1.5, facilities for merge tracking were introduced. With these new features, when you merge from one tree into another, the related revision numbers are stored.

You may be wondering what you can do with this information. Well, you can use it to avoid several problems as follows:

♦ **Avoiding repeated merges**: When a revision is marked as having been merged, future merges which are supposed to include that revision will skip over it, saving time and resources.

♦ **Improved traceability**: The log dialog now shows branch commits as part of the trunk log when a branch is merged back into the trunk, making it easier to follow changes.

♦ **Better blame**: Blame information now shows the person who made the changes, rather than the person who merged them, assuming that the check box for "include merge info" has been checked in the blame dialog.

Pop quiz – working with TortoiseSVN

1. Branches...

   a. Are what new releases are called in Subversion.

   b. Create more problems than they solve, and should be avoided at all costs.

   c. Can be used to allow different code streams to be worked on at the same time.

2. Merging...

   a. Frequently goes wrong, so should only be done when absolutely necessary.

   b. Is just like committing, and you can just click and forget.

   c. Should be done with care, and on a clean working copy.

3. Locking should be used:

   a. Files should be locked every night before you go home.

   b. On any file that you happen to be editing, to stop others from editing it.

   c. On files which are not trivially mergeable, such as audio, video, or complex document formats.

4. A tag:

   a. Acts like a snapshot—allowing you to go back to a specific revision in your project.

   b. Is a name you give your project so you can find it in the repo browser.

   c. Can only be created based on the HEAD revision.

5. To reduce the chances of problems with merges you should:

   a. Always use a clean working copy.

   b. Check that the results were as you expected as soon as the merge completes.

   c. Merge frequently.

   d. All of the above.

Summary

In this chapter you learned about branching, tagging, and merging. You learned why you would want to use these features (as well as some less-than-ideal examples of how they may be used), as well as how to avoid some of the conflicts that can occur during complex merges.

In this chapter you learned

- What branching is, and why you would want to use it
- What tagging is, and why you would want to use it
- How to create a branch
- How to switch your working copy
- How to merge one or more branches
- How to handle common conflicts

The examples in this chapter were quite simple, but they give you an idea of how to work with branches and tags, and how to handle the kinds of conflicts you are likely to encounter in the real world. Quinn and Mowbray can get away with eyeballing a folder to tell what a missing file has been renamed to, but you will most likely need to rely on the logs a lot more when you are working with a real world software project.

In the next chapter, you will learn how to keep your server tidy and organized—how to prune trees, and work with change lists and revision graphs. The next chapter will also discuss some other useful tools in Subversion, and explain how you can export a working copy, or relocate your working copy. These aren't things you are likely to need to do often, but the good news is that TortoiseSVN makes the task easy, should the need ever arise.

6
Working with Revision Logs

So far, you have learned how to create a working copy, submit changes (or a patch), synchronize those changes with the server, handle conflicts, and work with branches. We have touched on using the logs to find out what changes other developers have made to your code, but we have not explored the revision logs in depth. This chapter will explain **changelists**, **revision graphs**, *and other ways of tracking changes.*

In this chapter, we shall:

- ◆ Learn more about **differences**
- ◆ Learn about changelists
- ◆ Explore working with revision graphs
- ◆ Learn how to change **views** in revision graphs
- ◆ Learn how to prune **trees** to make the revision graph easier to understand

So let's get started...

Differences in detail

Differences are useful to allow you to see what has changed between recent revisions of a file. There are several different ways that you can view differences between files, or between a file and a previous version of the file.

Viewing differences between versions of a specific file in your working copy

In the previous chapters, you viewed differences using the change log. There is another way to view differences from within your working copy folder, using the right-click menu.

Time for action – viewing differences in a working copy

To view the differences between a file in your working copy and a previous version, follow these steps:

1. Navigate to your working copy folder.

2. Select the file that you want to compare version history for.

3. Right-click the file, and select **TortoiseSVN** | **Diff with previous version**.

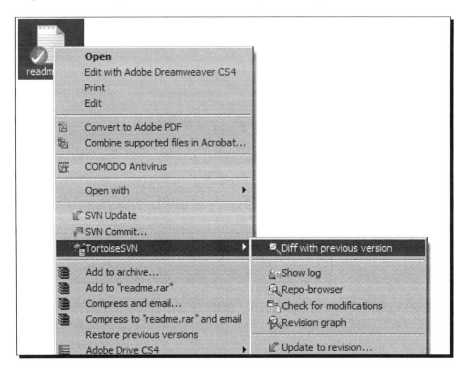

4. A **TortoiseMerge** window will appear, showing the differences between the current version of the file and the previous version.

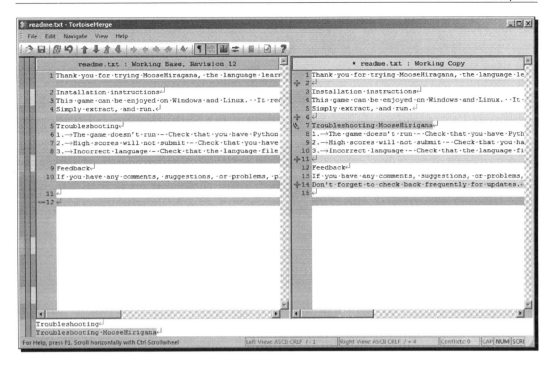

What just happened?

You have viewed the differences between a current version of a file and the previously checked in one. If you have made changes to a file, but not yet checked in those changes, you can view the difference between the BASE revision (the version that was in the repository when you last updated), and the working copy by selecting **TortoiseSVN | Diff**, instead of **TortoiseSVN | Diff with previous version**.

In addition to using this method, you can view specific differences by going to **TortoiseSVN | Show Log** and selecting the revision you are interested in from the list at the top of the window. Double-click on the relevant file in the list at the bottom of the window—this will bring up a **TortoiseMerge** window showing the difference list for the revisions in question.

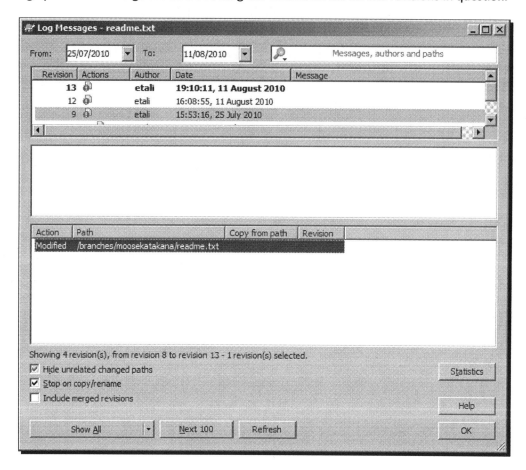

Viewing differences between files outside your working copy

You don't have to be inside your working copy to view differences. In fact, you can view differences between files that aren't under version control.

Time for action – viewing differences in files outside your working copy

To view the differences between files that aren't within your working copy:

1. Navigate to the folder where the files are stored.

2. Click on the older version of the file.

3. Hold down the *Ctrl* key and then click on the newer version of the file.

4. Right-click on the file, and select **TortoiseSVN | Diff**.

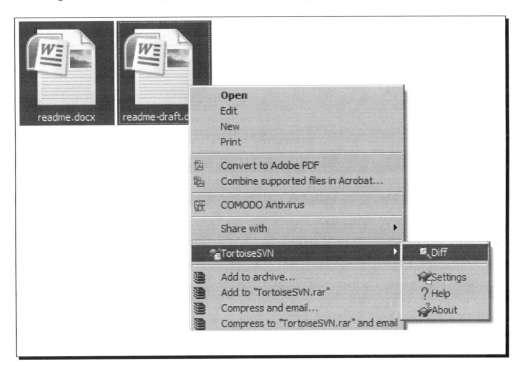

5. The next window will show the differences between the two files (depending on what applications you have installed, and the file type of the file you view the differences for, your screen may differ from the following screenshot):

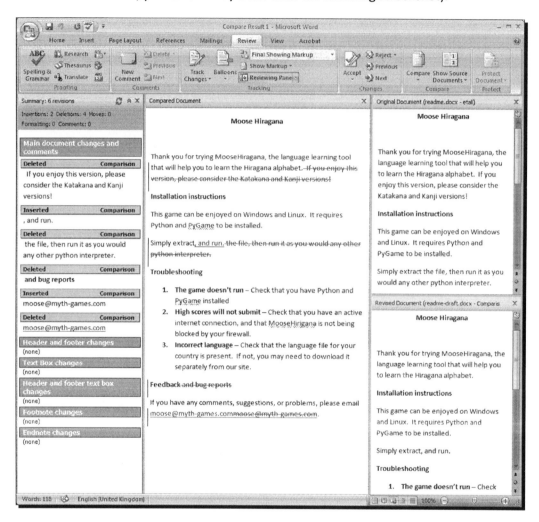

What just happened?

You have just viewed the differences between two files which are not under version control. You could use this to compare submitted patches, documents or source code. When you use this method to compare differences, the differences may be displayed in the editor or IDE that supports the file (as shown in the previous screenshot), or using the **TortoiseMerge** window:

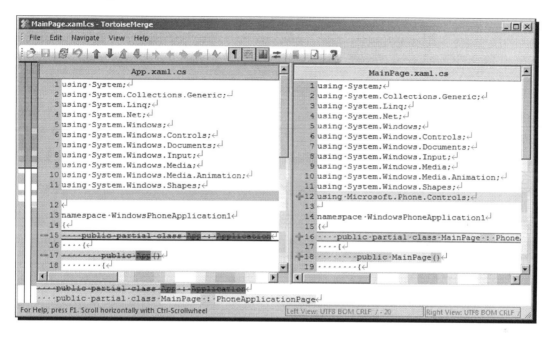

Comparing folders in the repository browser

If you want to make a bigger comparison, for example between two folders, you can use the repository browser to achieve this. Simply open the repository browser, right-click on one of the folders that you want to include in the comparison, and select **Mark for comparison**, then right-click on the second, and select **Show differences as a unified diff**:

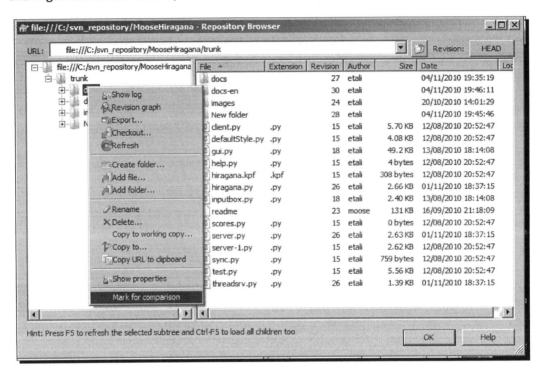

Comparing two folders is useful if you want to view the differences between several files that are in different folders. You get an at-a-glance comparison of each file.

Working with changelists

The best-case scenario for software development would be to work on one thing at a time, committing each change as you go. In the real world, however, things don't always work like that.

Quinn discovered that while attempting to make some network code changes, the current UI setup didn't have anywhere to display the network status. Being easily distracted, he decided to quickly create a status bar, and ended up tweaking some other parts of the UI too, before getting back to his network coding task. Before he even realized he'd gotten distracted, he had edited half the files in the project! Or so it felt when he saw the huge list in the commit window. Which file affects which task?

If Quinn was working on tasks which affected separate files, then he could group the files into **changelists**, separating those changelists according to task. This makes it easy for him to see what he is doing. He can commit the files related to UI changes by selecting the files in that changelist, and then later commit the network changes by selecting that changelist.

Sadly, this works well only if each task affects a different set of files. If one file is touched by more than one task, then you can't add that file to more than one changelist. Of course, that's a strong case for keeping your code as organized as possible!

Another important thing to remember is that changelists are stored on your local computer, rather than on the Subversion server. They're really a convenience tool for you, rather than a part of the version tracking. This means that you should still make sure to provide clear commit log messages so that other developers understand what is happening with each commit. Even small changes should be documented—your fellow developers will thank you for it, and you'll probably be glad of your log messages yourself a few months down the line!

Changelists are not available for Windows 2000.

If you're a user of Windows 2000, then you won't be able to take advantage of the Changelists feature in TortoiseSVN. Unfortunately, this feature is only available for Windows XP and above. If you're still using Windows 2000 after all these years, then it's likely that you will have encountered other applications that also have problems with the operating system. Perhaps now is a good time to ask your boss for an upgrade!

The first thing you need to learn is how to create a new changelist and add some files to it.

Time for action – working with changelists

To work with changelists, you will need to have worked on several different files before a commit. So before you proceed with this *Time for action*, modify several files within your working copy.

1. Navigate to your working copy.

2. Right-click inside the working copy folder and select **TortoiseSVN | Check for Modifications**.

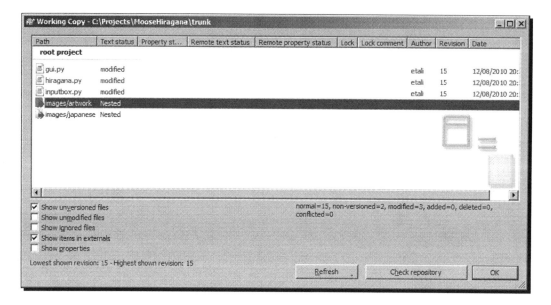

3. You will see that all of the modified files appear in the status list. This might be OK for relatively small commits, but could be confusing for bigger commits. To group the files into changelists, select the files in question, right-click on them, and then select **Move to changelist | <new changelist>**.

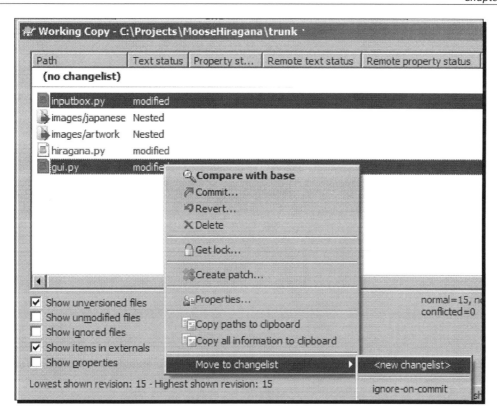

4. The **Create Changelist** window will appear. Enter a suitable name for your changelist.

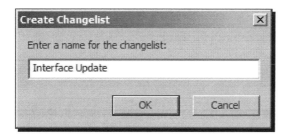

5. The files you have moved to the changelist will appear listed under that category. You can create as many changelists as you wish. The following screenshot shows two changelists for this particular commit:

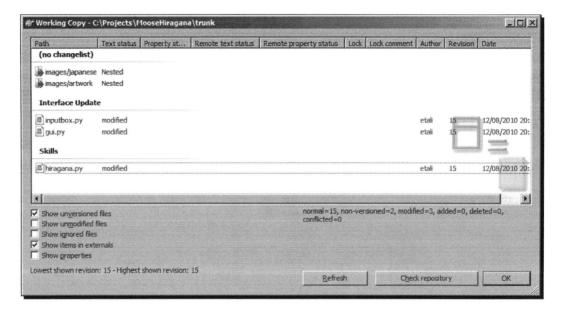

6. If you want to add a file to an already created changelist, simply right-click the file and select **Move to Changelist**, then click the name of the changelist in question.

What just happened?

You have learned how to create changelists. You can create more than one changelist, and you can add multiple files to each changelist. Once you have created a changelist, it will show in the right-click menu so that you can easily add files to it in the future.

Removing a file from a changelist

Just as you can add a file to a change list, it's possible to remove them too. Simply right-click on the file in question, and select **Remove from changelist**.

Ignoring files on commit

As mentioned previously, it's possible to tell TortoiseSVN to ignore files unless it is told otherwise. TortoiseSVN uses a special changelist for this called ignore-on-commit. If you add files to this changelist, then TortoiseSVN will ignore them in the future, even if the files have been modified locally.

This feature is useful for IDE project files – all developers probably have their own settings which they like to use, and there's no point synching their settings to the repository, as that would annoy the other developers on the team.

Working with revision graphs

Revision graphs provide an easy way for you to tell at-a-glance what is going on with your project. They provide a map, in easy-to-understand tree form, of the revision history of your project, including copies, branches, and tags.

One useful feature of revision graphs is that you can export them into a vector graphics format (WMF is a good option because they scale well and produce fairly small file size images. If you need a more widely supported format, then PNG is a good option) for inclusion with your source code, or on your project's website, giving everyone an easy overview of the status of your project.

You can view revision graphs for files, directories, or the whole project.

Time for action – viewing a revision graph

1. To view a revision graph, go to your working copy, and right-click inside the project, and then select **TortoiseSVN | Revision Graph**.

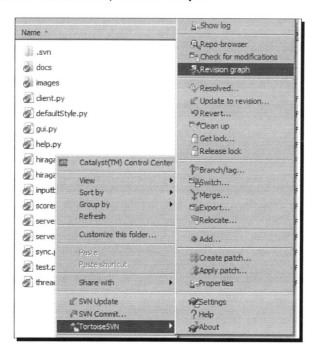

2. The graph that appears in the following screenshot shows the history of any branches and tags created, in an easy-to-understand, tree-like structure:

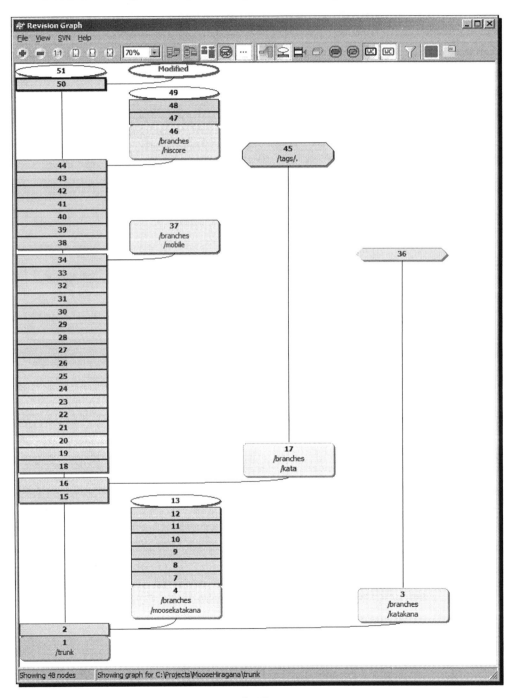

3. If you prefer to read from top to bottom, rather than having the newest node at the top of the screen, then click the **Show oldest node at top** button (this can be found two buttons to the right of the drop-down which allows you to change the zoom level). This will invert the view, as shown in the following screenshot:

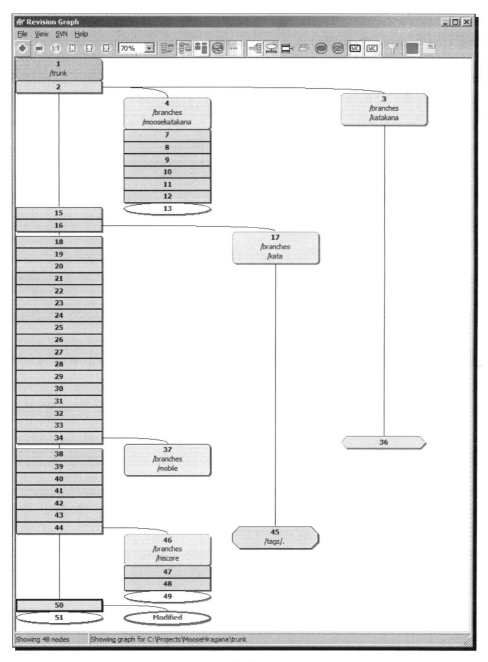

4. You can view information about a particular branch by right-clicking on it and selecting **Show Log**:

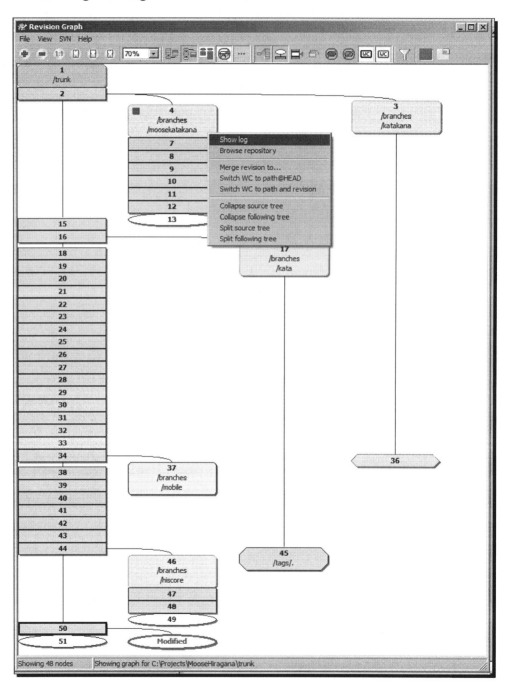

5. You can also use the same context menu to merge revisions, switch your working copy to a particular branch or tag, browse the repository, and collapse trees.

What just happened?

You have just used the revision graph to get an overview of the revisions, branches, and tags in your project. The last revision graph that we saw is a simple one, taken from our example project. In a real-world scenario, it is likely that the revision graph would be much more complex, and it is in these complex projects that having a revision graph becomes so useful.

When there are dozens of branches which are being created and merged, it can become difficult to keep track of what happened when, and why. A revision graph gives you a clear high-level view of everything that is happening in your software project.

To fully understand the revision graph, it helps to understand what each node means. The following table will help with this:

Item	Shape	Default Color
Items which have been added or copied	Rounded rectangle **1** /trunk	Green
Items which have been deleted		Red
Items which have been renamed		Blue
Branch HEAD revisions (if you have elected to show these)		Plain
Working copy revisions	Oval 19	Plain with bold outline (a red outline indicates modifications)
Modified working copies	Oval Modified	Plain with bold red outline

Item	Shape	Default Color
Moved items	Edged Rectangle	Blue

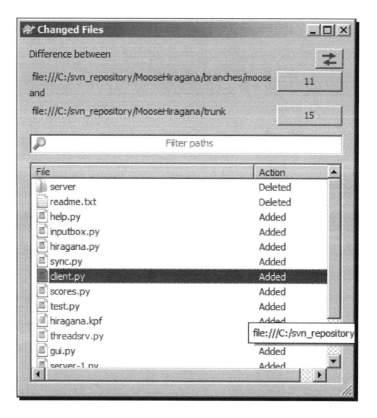

Item	Shape	Default Color
All other items	Rectangle	Plain

You can use the graph to get more detailed information about the differences between revisions. Just *Ctrl*-click on the two revisions you are interested in, right-click to bring up the context-sensitive menu, and then select **Compare Revisions.** You will be able to see a list of the revisions made to each file. Compare them using TortoiseDiff, as shown in the following screenshot:

You can also compare HEAD revisions, and view the unified differences using this method.

Changing your view

If your software project is quite large and complex, then you may find it useful to change the view used in the revision graph. There are several options that you can use to change the view you are using, and they can all be found under the view menu.

Rather than replicating the TortoiseSVN documentation by describing every single option, only the more interesting options will be described here. The other options are mostly clearly labelled, and otherwise are explained in the online help for TortoiseSVN:

- **Group by Branch**: This option is off by default, so all rows are sorted by revision. This can be a problem if you have branches with a long life and a few commits, because those branches will occupy a whole column, making the graph expand unnecessarily. This is demonstrated in the following screenshot:

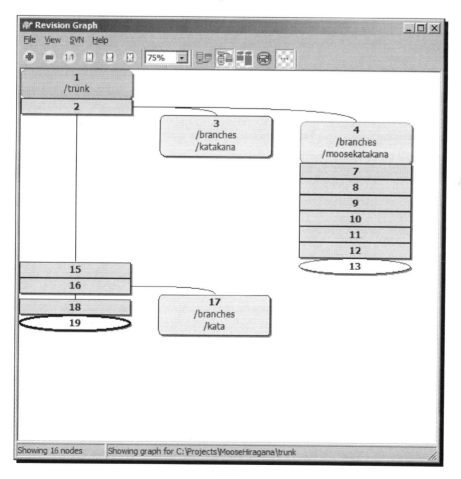

Turning on **Group by Branch** will change this so that revisions on a branch will be shown on consecutive lines, and branches will be grouped into columns, keeping the graph slim. The previous screenshot shows the default appearance of the revision graph (a shorter revision graph has been used here, for ease of viewing), the next screenshot shows the same revision graph with **Group by Branch**:

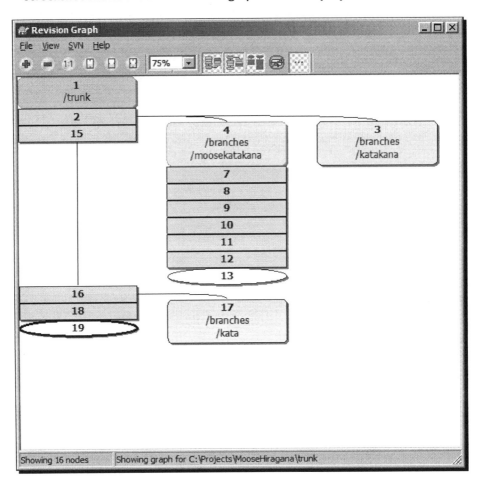

With this fairly simple tree layout, the difference isn't immediately clear, but if you have a lot of branches, you'll find that the group by branch feature keeps the layout much neater, and avoids needless scrolling.

◆ **Oldest on top**: This option switches the graph so that the oldest revisions are shown at the top of the screen. By default, the oldest revisions are at the bottom, and the 'tree' grows upwards.

◆ **Align trees on top**: This option forces trees to grow down, rather than appearing in their natural revision order, or aligned at the bottom of the window.

- ◆ **Reduce cross lines**: This option cleans up the revision graph if there are lots of crossing lines. In some cases, this option can make the layout appear less logical, and can also make the graph take up a larger area of the screen.

- ◆ **Differential path names**: This option makes the path names in the node boxes as short as possible—so if you create a branch called /branches/katakana/ images/characters out of /trunk/images/characters, the branch would be shown as merely /branches/katakana/.. the remainder of the path has not changed.

- ◆ **Exact copy sources**: The default behavior of the revision graph is to show branches as being taken from the last node where the change was made. In practice, many people make branches from the HEAD rather than from a specific revision. If you have a reason for needing to know which revision was used to create a copy, then you can use this option to show those details.

- ◆ **Fold tags**: If your project has a lot of tags, then you may find that they take up unnecessary screen space, hiding the information that you are interested in. You can use this option to hide the nodes for tags. If you still need to find a tag, you will find them displayed as tooltips on the node that they were copied from. Each source node that had a tag made from it will have an icon on the right-hand side indicating that a tag was made.

- ◆ **Tree stripes**: No, this option isn't related to landscape gardening. The tree stripes option tells TortoiseSVN to use alternating background colors so that it is easy to distinguish between different trees in the graph.

Keeping your view up-to-date

If you are viewing a revision graph of an active project, you may want to check for updates. Just as you would in your web browser, you can refresh the revision graph by pressing *F5*. This will connect you to the server (if you have been working offline) and check to see if there have been any new commits. Pressing *F5* to refresh works for most screens in TortoiseSVN. You can update your log dialog, for example, by pressing *F5* too.

Pop quiz – revision graphs

1. A revision graph is useful if:

   a. You are revising for a test.

   b. You want detailed statistics about every line of code changed in your project.

   c. You want a high-level overview of the branches, tags, and trees in your project.

2. By default, nodes are grouped by:

    a. Branch

    b. Revision

    c. Project

Pruning trees

Large software projects can end up with lots of trees. This can make the revision graph look excessively complex, and can make it harder for you to find the information that you need. The good news is that you can tame the trees in your graph, shrinking and expanding them as you need them.

To shrink a tree or a branch, simply hover your mouse over the point where the branch begins (where the node link enters the node), and you will be given the option to collapse the related tree (-), or expand it (+). If applicable, you will also be presented with the option to split a sub-tree into a separate graph (**x**), or re-attach a tree that had been split (**o**):

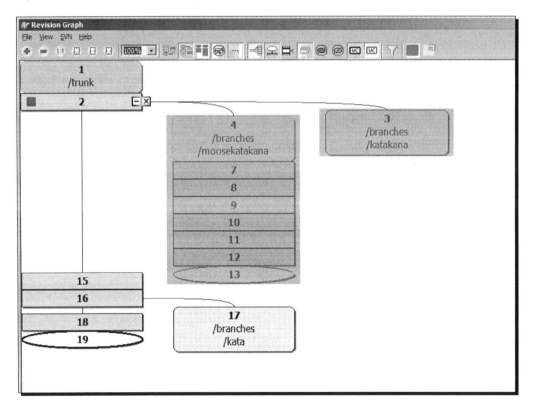

Pop quiz – working with your view

1. The Views menu allows you to:

   a. Decide whether the trees grow up or down

   b. Set whether to show HEAD revisions or not

   c. View the specific revision that a copy was made from

   d. All of the above

2. You can select multiple nodes in the revision graph using:

   a. The *Control* key

   b. The *Shift* key

   c. The middle mouse button

3. Change lists do not work on:

   a. All versions of Windows

   b. Windows Vista

   c. Windows 2000

Summary

In this chapter you learned how to view revision graphs, and how to manipulate your view of the graph to give a clearer view of the things that you are interested in.

In this chapter you learned:

- More ways to view differences
- How to view a revision graph
- How to manipulate the view to your tastes
- How to prune trees in the graph to make your view clearer
- How to add files to change lists

Revision graphs are useful for even small development teams. The good thing about the way TortoiseSVN displays them is that they are highly customizable, and scale well for larger projects. So, if you need to keep up with the lifecycle of branches and tags in a big project, then you can do so easily—thanks to the highly customizable views offered by TortoiseSVN!

In the next chapter, you will learn about exporting your working copy (to remove it from version control), and relocating your working copy, which you may need to do if the Subversion URL changes. The latter is something that you should not need to do often, but it is useful to know how to do it correctly, in case the need arises.

7

Exporting and Relocating Working Copies

So far you have learned how to create a working copy, submit changes (or a patch), synchronize those changes with the server, handle conflicts, work with branches, and understand changelists and revision logs. Sometimes you'll need to export the source code you're working on, and that's what this chapter will explain – how to export a working copy, or relocate your working copy if the need should arise.

In this chapter we shall:

- ♦ Learn how to **export** your working copy
- ♦ Learn how to **relocate** a working copy
- ♦ Learn how to **clean up** working copies
- ♦ Learn how to **troubleshoot** working copy errors

So let's get started...

Working with a working copy

Subversion is useful for development work, but there are times that you will want to have your project in its raw format. Subversion adds extra files and folders to your project, and if you are taking a backup of the project, or you want to put the raw source code on your website for people to download, then you will want to export the working copy so that you can get a clean version of the project, without the extra Subversion files.

Subversion adds some extra folders, with the name `.svn`, to each folder within your working copy. If you have not changed the default settings of Windows Explorer, then you may not be able to see those folders, but they are there, and if you were to simply copy or compress your working copy folder to share it with others.

If you have told Windows Explorer to show hidden files and folders, then inside each folder of your working copy you should see a grayed out folder with the name `.svn`.

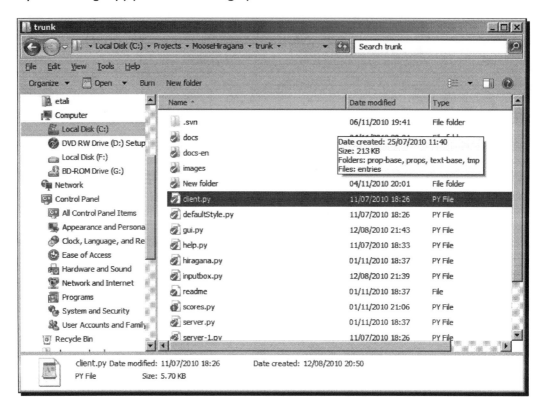

Inside that folder are several other folders containing information which is only useful for Subversion itself. Copying those files and folders would be a waste of storage space! The following screenshot displays the contents of the .svn folder:

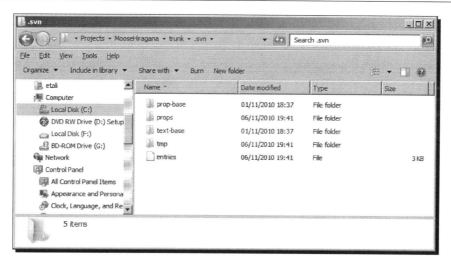

Exporting a working copy

Exporting a working copy gives you a "clean" version of the files in your project. To export your working copy, follow these steps:

Time for action – exporting a working copy

1. Navigate to your working copy folder.

2. Bring up the right-click context menu, and select **TortoiseSVN | Export...**.

3. A dialog box will appear asking you to select a folder. Choose where you would like to put your exported copy.

4. Click on **OK**. A window with a progress bar showing the progress of the export will appear.

5. Once the export is complete, navigate to the location of your exported files. You should see a clean, .svn folder free, version of your project, which can be archived, uploaded, or used as required.

What just happened?

You have just exported a working copy. This creates a copy of the files that are a part of your project, without the files that contain the version information. This is much easier, and faster, than making a copy manually and then deleting each .svn folder one by one.

In the previous example, it was assumed that you were exporting from your local hard drive. You can also export from a URL.

Exporting from a repository using a URL

TortoiseSVN behaves differently depending on where you execute the export command from.

Time for action – exporting from a URL

1. Navigate to the folder where you want your exported files to be stored.

2. Right-click inside the folder and select **TortoiseSVN | Export...**.

3. The **Export** dialog will appear.

4. Enter the URL to the repository, including the full path to the branch or trunk that you wish to export.

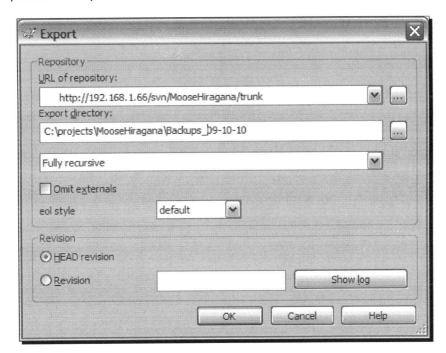

5. Click on **OK**, and the export will begin.

6. If the server has been set up to require authentication, you may be asked to enter a username and password.

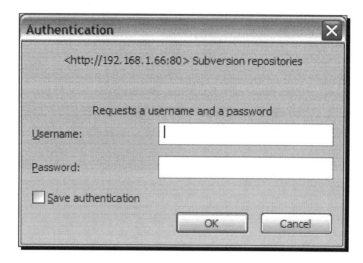

7. Once the export has completed, you will see a confirmation dialog.

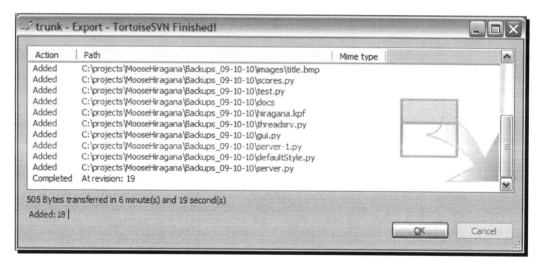

What just happened?

You have just exported a working copy from a remote Subversion server. You are likely to need to do this if you work for a large company, or are collaborating with people over the internet.

Sometimes you might want to remove the Subversion files and folders from your working copy. You could think of that as removing your working copy from version control. Fortunately, Tortoise SVN makes that easy.

Removing an existing working copy from version control

You can remove an existing working copy from version control by using the `export` command.

Time for action – removing an existing working copy from version control

1. Navigate to the working copy that you want to remove from version control.

2. Right-click on that working copy, and select **TortoiseSVN | Export...**

3. When prompted to select a path to export to, choose the working copy itself.

4. When the export completes, the `.svn` folders will have been removed from the working copy.

What just happened?

You have just removed a working copy from version control by exporting it onto itself. This might sound a little strange, but it works! TortoiseSVN detects that the source and destination for the export are the same, and skips the export process, simply removing the `.svn` folders instead.

Another way to remove a working copy from version control

You can achieve the same result in an easier way by right-clicking on a file, and dragging it onto itself. This is a rarely used shortcut – give it a try.

Time for action – removing a working copy from version control

1. Navigate to the working copy that you want to remove from version control.

2. Right-click on the folder in the right-hand pane in explorer.

3. While holding down the mouse button, drag the folder over to the left-hand pane, and drop it onto itself:

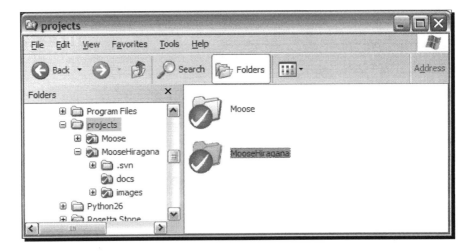

4. If you don't have the tree view in your explorer, you can achieve the same result by using two explorer windows and right-click dragging the folder from one to the other:

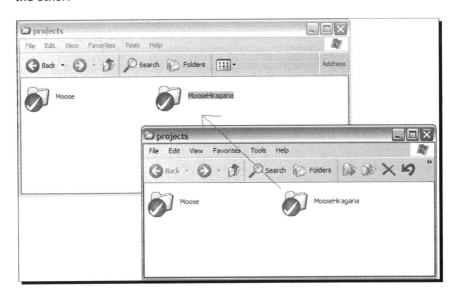

What just happened?

You have just used a shortcut to remove a working copy from version control. The end result is the same as with the first method, but this way is quicker and easier, and a nice shortcut to remember. Right-dragging files can be used for many different purposes in TortoiseSVN, and it is a good idea to familiarize yourself with them. For example, you can right-click and drag a non-versioned file into your Working Copy to be presented with the option to add it to version control. You can also drag files within your working copy to be offered the option to **SVN Move** or **SVN Copy** them, as the following screenshot demonstrates:

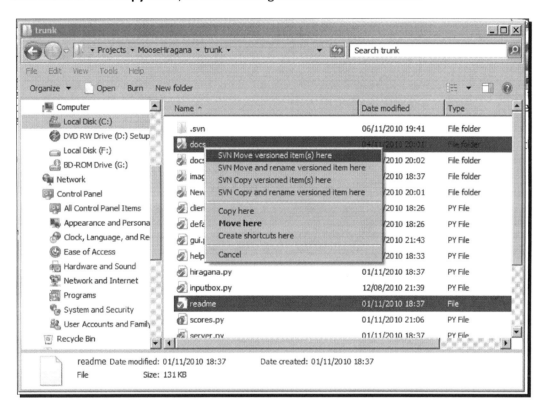

Changing to tree view in Windows XP

If you want to use tree view in Windows XP, simply click the **Folders** button at the top of the screen. This view is useful for developers who need to get a quick and easy overview of the layout of their projects, so you may decide that it is useful to make it the default.

Relocating your working copy

Sometimes you will need to relocate your working copy. This isn't something that you will need to do often, but it's still a good thing to know how to do. You may need to relocate your working copy if your Subversion server moves to a new URL, or changes IP address.

You could just check out again using the new address, but sometimes that isn't really the most convenient thing to do. For example, if you've made lots of changes, integrating your changes with the new working copy could be a long and drawn out process. That's why relocating your working copy is useful. It can save you a lot of time.

Imagine that Mowbray has been travelling, and while he was away he made a lot of changes to the source code for MooseHirigana. He gets back home to find out that Quinn has moved the Subversion server on to another part of the network with a different IP address.

Mowbray could check out the files from the repository manually, and then merge the changes by hand, but that would take a long time. It would be quicker, and easier, for him to change the repository path to the new one, and then commit the changes as normal.

Time for action – relocating your working copy

Relocating your working copy is made easy by TortoiseSVN:

1. Navigate to your working copy in explorer.

2. Right-click on the folder, and select **TortoiseSVN** | **Relocate**:

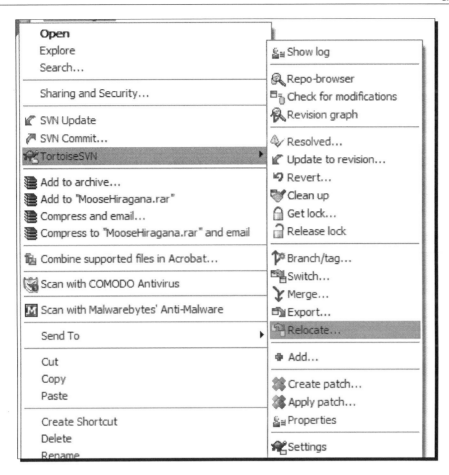

3. In the **Relocate** window that appears, enter the new path to the repository:

4. Click on **OK**.

5. If a password is required, you will be prompted for one. Enter it, and click **OK**.

6. The relocation process may take several minutes if your project is large.

What just happened?

You have just pointed your working copy to a different repository location. When you do this, Subversion changes all references to the old repository so that they point to the new one. The files in the working copy are unchanged. This means that Mowbray can now check in the changes that he made, as if nothing had changed while he was away.

Be careful when using the relocation option. You should use it only in cases where the repository address has changed. Using relocate at the wrong time could corrupt your working copy. A corrupt working copy is not a good thing! Sometimes you can fix corrupted working copies simply by performing a cleanup (as described later in this chapter), or by deleting the log file in the . svn folder and then attempting a cleanup, but in other cases you may find that your only reasonable recourse is to perform another checkout and painstakingly reproduce any changes you wanted to save.

To avoid such issues, a good rule to remember is this: If the first part of the URL (meaning the part that dictates the location of the repository) has changed, then you should use relocate.

If the organization inside the repository has changed, use switch instead.

As a real life example, imagine that Shiny Moose Software has an internal (intranet accessible only) repository located at http://shinymoose.local/repos/moosehirigana/trunk

If the company network administrator decided to change the repositories to be located on another intranet server, at http://repos.shinymoose.local/, then Quinn would need to use the relocate option to point to the new repository.

If the part of the path that changed was actually inside the repository (for example if /trunk were renamed to something else), then Quinn should use **relocate** rather than **switch**.

Recovering from a corrupt working copy

If you have made a lot of changes to your working copy and it becomes irrecoverably corrupt, then the BEYOND COMPARE utility may be of use. It integrates with Subversion (and other version control systems), and can be used to salvage the changes that you've made and merge them into a new working copy.

You can download BEYOND COMPARE from http://www.scootersoftware.com/index.php

Deleting a working copy

Once you've finished with a working copy, you will probably want to get rid of it – after all, there's no point cluttering up your hard drive with files for projects that you are no longer working on.

Deleting a working copy is a simple process. All you have to do is delete the folder on your hard drive. There's no need to tell Subversion that you're deleting the files. Simply get rid of them the way you would any other file on your hard drive.

Working copy cleanup

Sometimes you can run into problems where Subversion commands won't complete – perhaps the server has had issues, or perhaps some conflicts or other issues have caused problems. For example, if your IDE touched lots of files in your project – causing them to get a new timestamp, even though the files themselves haven't changed – then checkins could become an unnecessarily slow process.

To fix this, you can use the cleanup feature.

Time for action – executing a working copy cleanup

The cleanup feature can be found, as with other features, on the right-click context menu.

1. Navigate to your working copy.

2. Right-click inside the working copy folder and select **TortoiseSVN | Clean up**.

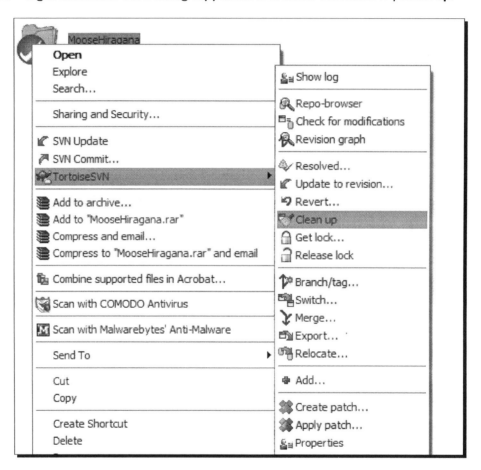

3. The cleanup process will begin. TortoiseSVN will fix any inconsistencies with your working copy. A progress bar will show how far along the process is.

4. Once it has completed, you will see a confirmation box, like the one shown in the following screenshot:

What just happened?

You have just used the TortoiseSVN cleanup feature to fix any inconsistencies in your working copy. In the case of the timestamp example given at the start of this section, the SVN server will now have the new timestamps. The cleanup feature should fix most problems and inconsistencies that you are likely to encounter. The cleanup feature works because Subversion tries to make updates as safe as possible. Before it changes anything in your working copy, it writes a record of the changes to a log file. If the update fails for any reason (for example if the computer crashes, or the process is terminated) then Subversion can go through the log files and attempt to complete the update, getting the working copy back into a consistent state.

Cleanup can be used to fix aborted commits, failed commits, and, in some cases, corrupt files in the .svn folder.

Troubleshooting working copy problems

Most of the time, Subversion handles things smoothly, and if you do run into a problem, then either executing a cleanup or using the conflict resolution option will solve the issue.

However, sometimes you can encounter issues that require a different solution.

A few of those are:

Folders have a red exclamation mark, despite nothing having changed

This sometimes happens simply because Windows Explorer has gotten out of sync. Clicking *Ctrl+F5* to refresh the view in explorer can fix this. This issue is particularly common if you have just performed a commit on a working copy, because explorer does not update its views very often.

If *Ctrl+F5* does not fix the problem, then try using the context menu, selecting **TortoiseSVN | Check for modifications**. You may find that there is a hidden file there that you need to commit. To avoid missing hidden files in the future, consider setting Windows Explorer to show hidden files.

Certain context menus are missing from inside my working copy

TortoiseSVN is an extension of Windows Explorer. If Windows Explorer crashes or encounters a problem, then this can sometimes cause it, and therefore TortoiseSVN, to behave strangely. If your view is messed up, or certain context menus are missing, then restarting Explorer can often fix the problem.

To restart Windows Explorer, open **Task Manager** and look for `explorer.exe` in the process list. Select it, and then click **End Process**.

Next, go to **File | New Task**, type in explorer.exe and then click **OK**.

Logging out of Windows and then back in, or rebooting, is another common way of solving Windows Explorer problems.

Access denied errors

This error appears if you try to commit files a project that you do not have correct permissions for. If you get this error, and you believe that you should be able to commit files to a project, first check that you have entered the correct credentials. If the problem persists, contact the manager of the Subversion server.

Changing the case of a file name doesn't work

Subversion has its roots in Linux, which is a case-sensitive family of operating systems. Windows-based operating systems are case-insensitive; this causes lots of trouble when you try to change the case of a filename.

If you simply attempt to change `Readme` to `README` in the file name, then this will not work – Subversion expects both files to exist, but Windows thinks they're the same file, which causes problems.

There are several workarounds for this issue, but the easiest is to do the following:

Time for action – changing the case of a file name

1. Commit any recent changes to the repository.

2. Open the TortoiseSVN repo browser.

3. Right-click on the file you want to change the case of, and select **Rename**. Give it the correctly capitalized file name.

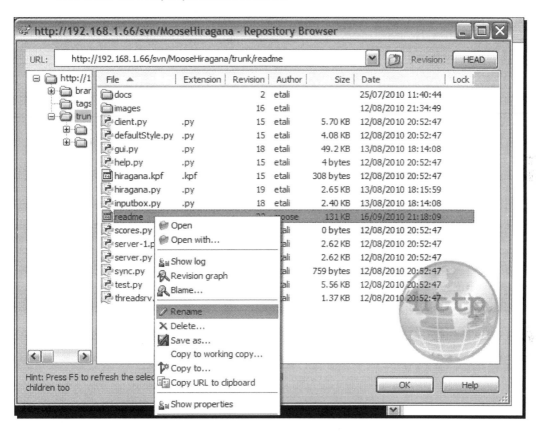

4. Enter a log message when you are prompted.

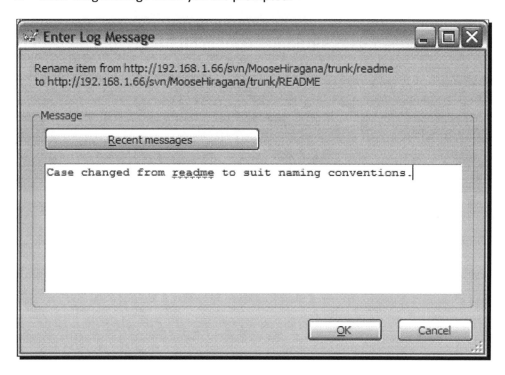

5. Click on **OK**.

6. Finally, check for updates on your working copy, to download the renamed version of the file.

What just happened?

You have worked around the problem of case-insensitivity on Windows-based operating systems by renaming the file on the server and downloading the change. This allows you to change the case of a file name without running into any OS related problems.

My computer becomes sluggish when I right-click on a file

Right-clicking on a file can sometimes cause performance problems on Windows XP. This is because of a bug which can cause Windows XP to have 100% CPU usage while the right-click menu is being displayed.

This issue does not affect everyone, but if it affects you, then the good news is that there is a relatively simple fix.

To prevent Windows XP from going to 100% CPU usage when you right-click on a file, disable the GUI transition effects.

You can do this by going to the Control Panel and selecting the **Appearance** tab, then going to **Effects** and unchecking the **Use the following transition effect for menus and tooltips box**. Once you have done this, click **OK**.

If you prefer to have the transition effects enabled, then another workaround is to left click on the file or folder you are interested in to select it before right-clicking on it to bring up the context-sensitive menu.

Pop quiz – working with your working copy

1. You would relocate your working copy if:

   a. You wanted to store it in another folder on your hard drive

   b. You needed to take a backup of it

   c. Your Subversion server moved to another URL or IP address

   d. All of the above

2. You would export your working copy if:

   a. You wanted to publish the clean source code on the web

   b. You wanted to take a backup of the files without the extra `.svn` folders

   c. You wanted to remove the working copy from version control

   d. All of the above

3. Deleting a working copy can be done via:

   a. Windows Explorer

   b. TortoiseSVN

   c. The repo browser

Summary

This chapter looked at how to export and relocate working copies, and how to troubleshoot some of the issues that you might encounter while using TortoiseSVN.

In this chapter you learned:

- How to relocate a working copy
- How to export a working copy
- How to remove a working copy from version control
- How to troubleshoot common issues and errors

Exporting a working copy is useful for backup purposes, and also to allow you to post a clean version of your source code on the web. Hopefully you won't need to use the knowledge of relocating working copies too often, but for those rare occasions where your network is restructured, the knowledge will be useful.

In the next chapter, you will learn how to use **SubWCRev**, a keyword substitution tool that makes it easy for you to perform batch updates on keywords — for example to replace the version number of your program in all documentation, help, and about screens.

8

Keyword Substitution with SubWCRev

Up until now you have learned how to create a working copy, submit changes (or a patch), handle conflicts, work with branches, changelists, and revision logs, and how to export or move your working copy. This chapter will cover **SubWCRev**, *a tool which allows you to automate the replacement of text throughout files in your project, making it easy to update files with the correct version number, or other details, in one go.*

In this chapter we shall:

- ◆ Learn how to use SubWCRev via the command line
- ◆ Learn the keyword substitution switches
- ◆ Learn how to use the COM interface
- ◆ Learn how to set up Pre-build events in your IDE

So let's get started...

Why use SubWCRev?

MooseHiragana is a frequently updated piece of software. To make it easier for people providing technical support, users are asked to include what version of the software they are using in their support requests. The version number is listed on the **About** page of the software, and is also given on the startup screen, and in the documentation.

That's three different places that need to be updated every time a new revision is released. It would be easy for a developer to forget to update one of those, or to make a mistake and end up having different numbers showing on the about page, in the help files, and on the startup screen. That wouldn't look very professional!

SubWCRev can be used to save time and ensure that all pages are updated with accurate information. SubWCRev finds the highest revision that the working copy is on and treats that as the revision number to be used. This isn't always correct, but in most cases, it's exactly what is wanted!

Using SubWCRev via the command line

SubWCRev is a useful Subversion tool. It reads the Subversion status of all files in a working copy, and then records the highest commit revision number, along with that revision's timestamp, and whether there are any local modifications in that revision.

You can call SubWCRev via the command-line, or from a script.

Time for action – exporting a working copy

To use SubWCRev from the command line:

1. Create a file that you would like to use as a template for your revision information document. In this case, we've decided to call the file `hiragana.tmpl`.

2. Put the following text into that file:

   ```
   Moose Hiragana:  The Japanese Learning Game
   Brought to you by Shiny Moose Software

   Revision: $WCREV$
   Modified: $WCMODS?Yes:No$
   Date: $WCDATE$
   Range: $WCRANGE$
   URL: $WCURL$
   Lock Status: $WCISLOCKED?Locked:Not Locked$
   Locked By: $WCLOCKOWNER$
   ```

3. Open a command-line window, navigate to where the template file has been saved, and enter the following command (substituting PATH\TO\WORKING-COPY with the full path to your working copy):

   ```
   Subwcrev.exe PATH\TO\WORKING-COPY hiragana.tmpl hiragana.txt
   ```

4. You should see some text similar to the following (with the applicable revision numbers and paths):

```
SubWCRev: 'c:\projects\moosehiragana'
Last committed at revision 43
Updated to revision 43
```

5. A file called `hiragana.txt` will have appeared in the folder. Open it, and you should see something similar to the following:

```
Moose Hirigana:  The Japanese Learning Game
Brought to you by Shiny Moose Software

Revision: 43
Modified: No
Date: 2010/07/11 18:31:57
Range: 43
URL: http://192.168.1.66/svn/MooseHiragana
Lock Status: Not Locked
Locked By:
```

What just happened?

You have just used the command-line to run `SubWCRev.exe`, to update a file called `hiragana.txt` with the latest information about the project, based on a template.

The template shown was quite simple, but it shows how useful SubWCRev can be. Imagine if you had to re-enter all that information by hand with each new build!

If you ran into problems following the above steps, make sure that you entered the paths for each file correctly. If you run SubWCRev from the location where the `.tmpl` file is stored, you do not need to enter the correct path.

You could use these commands to update the text for version information the **About** page, and in the documentation too.

Don't forget to exclude the text file from versioning. The template file can be versioned, but if the text file is versioned then you will be expected to commit the changes every time you generate a new version of the file.

SubWCRev can only be used on a working copy

It is important to note that SubWCRev can only be used on a working copy. You cannot use it directly on the repository.

Pop quiz – getting to grips with SubWCRev

1. SubWCRev uses templates to:

   a. Avoid problems with version control – the template is versioned, the output is excluded

   b. Avoid problems with version control, the output is versioned, the template is excluded

   c. Make it easy to copy and edit files as required

2. You can use SubWCRev:

   a. On the working copy

   b. On the repository

   c. On either

Have a go hero – updating documentation

The documentation for MooseHiragana mentions the current version number in several places. Each time there is a major update, a staff member goes through the documentation and updates it to reflect things that have been added, altered, or removed. However, despite the application being fairly simple, it's easy to miss references to a version number in all the text.

SubWCRev is an ideal solution to this problem. There are two help files, a simple 'getting started' in the form of a text file called README, and a more in-depth HiraganaHelp.html. How could SubWCRev be used to solve this problem?

Command-line switches

SubWCRev has a number of optional switches which can be used individually, or in groups.

Switch	Usage
-d	This switch will cause SubWCRev to exit with ERRORLEVEL 9 if the destination file exists. The destination file will not be modified at all. You should use this option if your IDE detects the date a file has changed, and you want to prevent your IDE from erroneously doing a full rebuild.
-e	This switch tells SubWCRev to examine directories which have been included via svn:externals, if they are from the same repository. This differs from the default behavior, which is to ignore externals.
-f	This switch tells SubWCRev to include the most recent revisions of folders. This differs from the default behavior, which is to use only the revision numbers of files.
-m	This switch will cause SubWCRev to exit with ERRORLEVEL 8 if the working copy has mixed revisions. This switch can be used to prevent a build from taking place if the working copy is only partially updated.
-n	This switch will cause SubWCRev to exit with ERRORLEVEL 7 if the working copy contains local modifications. This switch can be used to prevent a build from taking place if there are uncommitted changes in the working copy.
-x	This switch tells SubWCRev to write revision numbers in hexadecimal.
-X	This switch tells SubWCRev to write revision numbers in hexadecimal, prepending 0X.

The use of some of the above command-line switches may not be immediately clear, but you will soon see how they can be useful, when we look at using SubWCRev with build events.

Using command-line switches

To use a group of command-line switches, you must specify them all together. For example, -fX will work, but -f -X will not.

Keyword substitution switches

SubWCRev can be used to add several different pieces of information, including the current date and time, details of file locks, commit revision numbers and the URL of the repository.

Keyword	Usage
$WCREV$	This is replaced with the highest commit revision in the working copy.
$WCDATE$	This is replaced with the commit date and time of the highest commit revision. The default date format is `yyyy-mm-dd hh:mm:ss`. You can specify a custom format if you wish.
$WCNOW$	This is replaced with the current system date and time. You can use this switch to record the build time. You can specify a custom date format if you wish.
$WCRANGE$	This is replaced with the update revision range in the working copy. In most cases, this will be replaced with a single revision. However, if the current working copy has mixed revisions, then a range will appear here in the format of 123:456
$WCMIXED$	This will be replaced by one set of text if there are mixed update revisions, and another if there are not.
$WCMODS$	This will be replaced by one string if there are local modification and another if there are not.
$WCURLS$	This is replaced by the URL of the repository associated with the working copy.
$WCINSVN$	This is replaced by one string if the entry is versioned, and another if it is not.
$WCNEEDSLOCK$	This is replaced by one string if the `svn:needs-lock` property is set, and another if it is not.
$WCISLOCKED$	This is replaced by one string if the entry is locked, and another if it is not.
$WCLOCKDATE$	This is replaced with the date that the lock was done. You can format this however you wish.
$WCLOCKOWNER$	This is replaced with the name of the person who owns the lock.
$WCLOCKCOMMENT$	This is replaced with any lock comments.

Some substitutions are for files only

Some of the above substitutions are for single files, rather than an entire working copy. These switches are $WCLOCKDATES$, $WCLOCKOWNERS$, $WCISVN$, $WCNEEDSLOCKS$, $WCISLOCKED$, and $WCLOCKCOMMENTS$.

Mixed revisions, modifications, and status

In the previous table, there are several keyword substitution switches which are substituted with one string if something is true, and another if the specified condition is false.

To use these in your templates, use the following syntax:

```
Lock Status: $WCISLOCKED?TextIfLocked:TextIfNotLocked$
```

Setting a custom date format

As mentioned earlier, the default date format used by SubWCRev is: `yyyy-mm-dd hh:mm:ss`.

To specify a custom format, use the following syntax: `$WCDATE=%a %d %B %I:%M:%S %p$`.

The full list of codes is shown in the following table:

Code	Usage
%a	Short weekday name – example, Mon
%A	Full weekday name – example, Monday
%b	Short month name – example, Jan
%B	Full month name – example, January
%c	Standard date and time
%d	Day of the month – number from 1-31
%H	Hour, in 24 hour format (00-23)
%I	Hour, in 12 hour format (1-12)
%j	Day of the year, in number format (1-366)
%m	Month, as a number (1-12)
%M	Minute, as a number (0-59)
%p	AM or PM (or the localized version of this)
%S	Second, as a number (0-59)
%U	Week of the year, as a number (0-53). Week 1 has the first Sunday
%w	Weekday as a number (0-6). Sunday is 0
%W	Week of the year (0-53). Week 1 has the first Monday
%x	Standard date string
%X	Standard time string
%y	The year as a number, without the century (0-99)
%Y	The year as a number, with the century

Code	Usage
%Z	The name of the time zone
%%	A percentage sign

Pop quiz – keyword substitution switches

1. Keyword substitution switches

    a. Are used in the template to dictate where text goes

    b. Are used to switch SubWCRev on and off

    c. Are used in the output, to indicate where SubWCRev has made changes

2. Which of the following is not a keyword substitution switch:

    a. $WCISLOCKED$

    b. $WCLOCKSTATUS$

    c. $WCRANGE$

    d. $WCMIXED$

3. When changing the format of the output used by SubWCRev for dates, which of the following is not a valid option:

    a. %U

    b. %s

    c. %e

    d. %Z

Using the COM interface

There may be occasions where you need to access Subversion revision information from within other programs. To do this, you can use SubWCRev's COM interface.

Create an object called SubWCRev.object, and use the following methods:

Method	Usage
.Author	Returns the author that last committed changes to the working copy.
.Date	Returns the date and time of the highest commit revision.
.GetWCInfo	Use this method to gather revision information from the working copy. You must call this method before calling the other methods in this list.
.HasModifications	This method returns true if there are local modifications.

Method	Usage
.IsLocked	This method returns true if the item is locked.
.IsSvnItem	This method returns true if the item is versioned.
.LockCreationDate	This method returns the date when the lock was created. If there is no lock, it returns an empty string.
.LockComment	This method returns the message that was entered when the lock was created.
.LockOwner	This method returns the name of the lock owner. If there is no lock owner, it returns an empty string.
.MaxRev	This method returns the maximum update revision from $WCRANGE$.
.MinRev	This method returns the minimum update revision, as shown in $WCRANGE$
.NeedsLocking	This method returns true if svn:needs-lock is set.
.URL	This method returns the repository URL of the working copy.

You can use the COM interface to pull SVN information using other applications – for example MS Word or Excel. This makes it a great time-saver when you're writing reports, documentation, or team updates.

An example of reading Subversion keywords from within MS Word can be found at http://insights.oetiker.ch/windows/SvnProperties4MSOffice.html. At the time of writing, the source code links were dead, so I have mirrored the code samples on my blog at: http://lesleyharrison.wordpress.com/2010/11/14/subversion-keywords-and-tortoisesvn/. The above listed information can be accessed and parsed into a Word document, or an Excel file, making it ideal for reporting purposes – if you want to see which files are being changed or locked and who was responsible for touching them, then this is the ideal way.

You will need to have macros enabled in MS Office in order to be able to use the above example code. The Macro settings can be found by clicking the Office Button and going to **Word Options | Trust Center** and clicking **Trust Center Settings....** then selecting **Macro Settings**. I would not recommend enabling all Macros, as this leaves you open to malicious macros. The best option is to allow macros to run with notification only.

A detailed explanation of the use of the COM interface is beyond the scope of this book; however, if you would like to know more about using COM interface, then I recommend you experiment with the sample script which can be found at:

http://code.google.com/p/tortoisesvn/source/browse/trunk/src/
SubWCRev/testCOM.js

Using SubWCRev as a pre-build event in your IDE

As you have already seen, SubWCRev is a great time-saver. When you run SubWCRev, it will automatically substitute certain pieces of information into the files that it is told to look at.

However, running it manually is a pain, and Quinn often forgets to run it when he does a major build. To make sure that the information in `hiragana.txt` is always up-to-date, Quinn decides to automate the process.

The way that you set up a pre-build event will depend on the IDE that you are using. Some of the more popular IDE's options are described below.

Time for action – pre-build events in Visual Studio C++ applications

To add a pre-build event in Visual Studio:

1. Open your project in Visual Studio.

2. Go to **Project | PROJECTNAME** properties (Where PROJECTNAME is the name of your project.

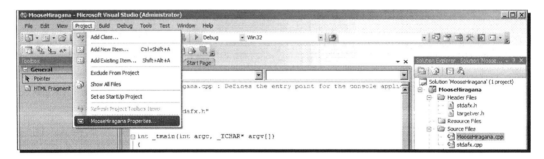

3. In the window that appears, select **Configuration Properties | Build Events | Pre-Build Event**.

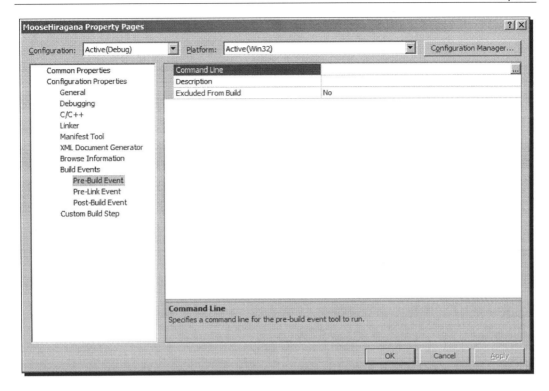

4. Enter the command-line information that you want to use to run SubWCRev – this should be similar to the information you entered in the first section about running the files from the command line.

5. Click **Apply**, and then build your project.

6. If everything is set up correctly, then SubWCRev will run, and then the project will build.

7. If for any reason SubWCRev returns an error, then the build will fail.

What just happened?

You have just set up Visual Studio C++ Application pre-build event. Now each time you build your application, SubWCRev will run. If SubWCRev succeeds, the build will continue. If SubWCRev returns an error, the build will be aborted.

You can use the command-line switches mentioned earlier in the chapter (the switches –d, –m, and –n) to ensure that the build is aborted if there are issues with the working copy. Remember that if you want to use more than one of those switches, you should group them together rather than adding them one by one to the command.

Now that SubWCRev runs automatically on each build, Quinn can be sure that all the files that need to be updated are being updated each time he does a build. So there's no need to worry about out of date documentation or loading screens — at least not for the things that SubWCRev can manage. If only SubWCRev could write the rest of the manual too!

Time for action – pre-build events in Visual Studio C# applications

1. In **Solution Explorer**, select your project.

2. Go to **Project | PROJECTNAME** properties (Where **PROJECTNAME** is the name of your project).

3. Select **Build Events**.

4. Enter the command to be run in the **Pre-build event command line:** text box.

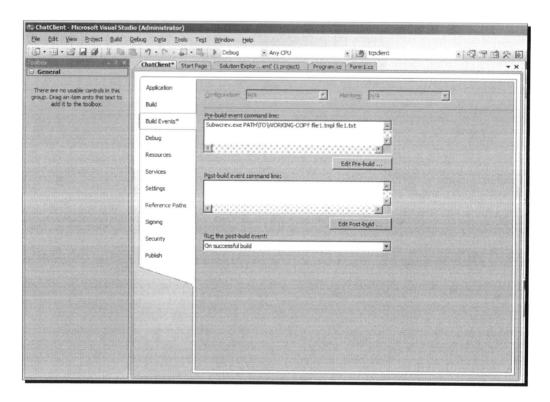

5. You can enter the pre-build information in this box, or, click **Edit-Pre Build...** to get a better edit box.

6. Clicking **Macros** will give you more information about project paths, which you may find helpful when writing your pre-build commands.

7. Once you have completed these steps you can build your project. If everything is set up correctly, SubWCRev will run and then the project will build. Otherwise, SubWCRev will return an error, and the build will fail.

What just happened?

You have just successfully set up a pre-build event for a C# project. Now that you have this set up, when you successfully build the project, SubWCRev will run. If the project does not build correctly, the event will not run.

Time for action – pre-build events in Visual Studio VB applications

Creating a pre-build event for Visual Basic is similar to creating one for C++:

1. Open your project in Visual Studio.

2. Go to **Projects | PROJECTNAME Properties** (Where **PROJECTNAME** is the name of your project):

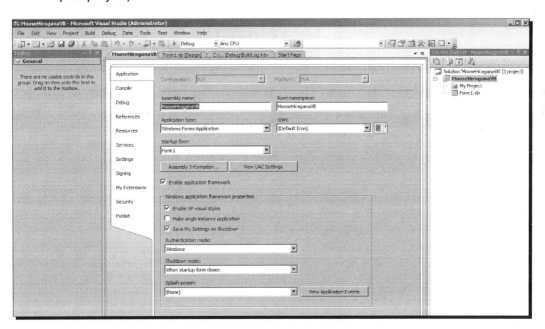

3. Select **Compile**.

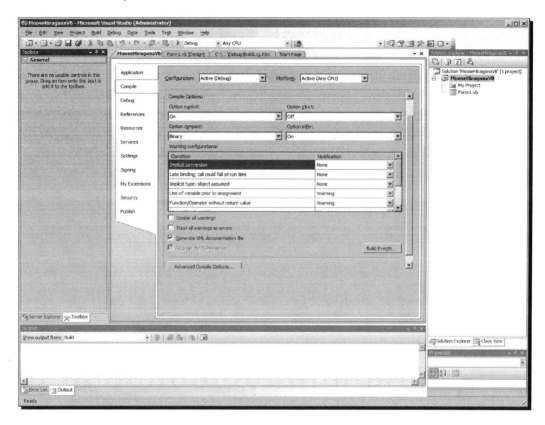

4. Click the **Build Events...** button (you may need to scroll down to find this).

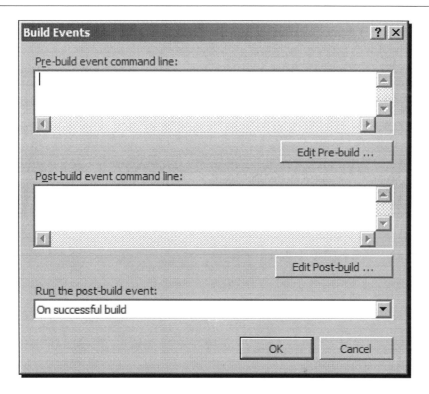

5. You can enter the pre-build information in this box, or, click **Edit-Pre Build...** to get a better edit box:

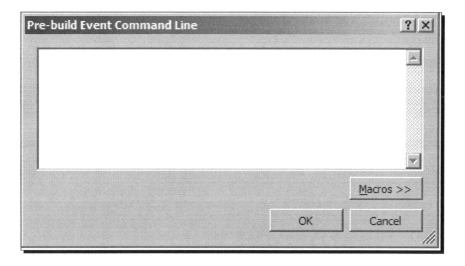

6. Clicking **Macros** will give you more information about project paths, which you may find helpful when writing your pre-build commands:

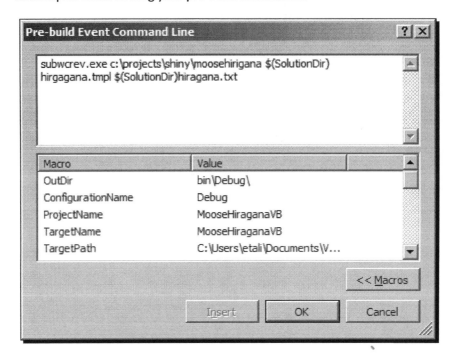

7. Once you have done this, build your project. If everything is set up correctly, SubWCRev will run and then the project will build. Otherwise, SubWCRev will return an error, and the build will fail.

What just happened?

You have successfully set up a pre-build event for a Visual Basic project. Now that you have this set up, when you build the project, SubWCRev will run.

If you want SubWCRev to prevent a build from taking place under certain conditions, you can tell it to return an error when those conditions are met, by using the command-line switches mentioned earlier in this chapter. To add one of the command-line switches to your command, just put them at the end of the line, like this:

```
SubWCRev.exe PATHTOWORKINGCOPY TEMPLATEFILE OUTPUTFILE -SWITCHES
```

Time for action – build events in Eclipse

1. Open your project in Eclipse.

2. Go to **Project | Properties**.

3. In the **Properties** window that appears, select **C/C++ Build | Settings**.

4. Select the **Build Steps** tab, and enter your pre-build commands (as discussed in the command line section of this chapter) in the Command: box under Pre-Build steps.

5. Click **Apply** to save your configuration.

What just happened?

You have now defined a pre-build step in Eclipse. The pre-build step will be run when you build your project. The pre-build step is not executed if the main build is found to be up to date; it will be executed only if a build takes place.

Using pre-build events with other IDEs

You can use pre-build events with most IDEs. If you're a notepad-style developer then you could even create your own makeshift pre-build events using batch files or Perl. The beauty of SubWCRev is that it is so easy to use on the fly.

Covering every IDE in existence is far beyond the scope of this book; however the documentation for your IDE should cover the topic of pre-build commands in depth.

Pop quiz – keyword substitution

1. Keyword substitution is used to:

    a. Port your program to another programming language.

    b. Translate your program into another language.

    c. Update certain Subversion related information such as version number and lock status.

    d. All of the above.

2. You can run SubWCRev:

    a. From the command line.

    b. As a pre-build event in your IDE.

    c. All of the above.

3. The date and time format used by SubWCRev:

   a. Is fixed as `dd-mm-yy hh-mm-ss`.

   b. Is fixed to `dd-mmm-yyy hh-mm-ss`.

   c. Can be customized.

Summary

This chapter looked at how to use SubWCRev to automate the replacement of important build information in files.

In this chapter you learned:

- What SubWCRev can do
- How to run SubWCRev from the command-line
- What the switches for SubWCRev are
- How to run SubWCRev as a pre-build event in your IDE

SubWCRev is a great time saver, and can be used to automate replacing build information across one or more files in your project.

In the next chapter you will learn how to use TortoiseSVN with Bug Tracking Systems, including `Trac`, `Google Projects`, `Redmine`, and `Jira`.

9
Using TortoiseSVN with Bug Tracking Systems

Unless your program is a trivial one—more like a script than a full application—it's guaranteed that it will evolve over time as you find issues with it, and, once it is released, your users will find bugs too.

Most teams use an issue tracker to monitor these problems, prioritizing bugs based on how serious they are, and how many users are affected by them. It is possible to integrate TortoiseSVN with many different issue trackers, making it easy to link the commits you and your team make to the issues that they relate to.

In this chapter, we shall see how to integrate TortoiseSVN with:

- ◆ Trac
- ◆ Google Projects
- ◆ Redmine
- ◆ Jira
- ◆ Other issue trackers

So let's get started...

Why use bug trackers?

If your usual development work involves banging out a script or a small plugin over the course of a weekend, then you're probably not used to using a formal bug tracking system. With small projects, you can get away with writing a few lines, testing them, fixing any problems, then repeating the process until you reach the stage you want. You can keep a running list of bugs in your head.

With bigger projects—or projects with more than a couple of developers—the list of bugs is going to get bigger, and the person who discovers the problem may not always be the person who can fix it. Once you reach the stage of releasing software—and taking bug reports from users, you definitely need an easy way to keep track of bugs.

Let's imagine that Quinn decides to release an Alpha build of MooseHiragana. The build has worked well during internal testing, but it turns out that it's not quite ready for the real world. The server has not been tested with anything more than five users connected. For that matter, the game hasn't been tested over the internet at all, so the network code, which works great over the LAN, simply is not ready for the laggy conditions of the internet. When a few hundred eager users try to connect at the same time, strange things start happening. Sometimes the game crashes, sometimes scores are posted incorrectly, sometimes it just becomes incredibly slow. It doesn't take long for the server to run out of memory and keel over completely, at which point any user attempting to play the multiplayer time-attack version of MooseHiragana will find that their game crashes.

A company that doesn't use bug tracking software would be in for a nasty surprise at this point. Their users wouldn't know where to turn, so they'd flood the game's forums, and the support e-mail address, with complaints and questions. As they don't have the benefit of a recommended format for a bug report, they won't know what information is needed, so the e-mails are likely to be next to useless in terms of troubleshooting information.

Fortunately, Shiny Moose Software uses a bug tracking system; in this case, Google Code, and has prominent links to the project page on their website, in the documentation, and within the game. Users who are having problems are directed to the project so they can look for help on the wiki, and report issues in the issue tracker.

Mowbray has created an issue template which asks users several questions that are likely to be relevant in a typical bug report. Most users at least attempt to answer the questions, and this greatly improves the quality of the bug reports compared to randomly fired-off e-mails. The template looks like this:

```
Describe the steps to replicate the problem.

What do you expect to happen? What happens instead?

What edition of the product are you using? (For example, netbook, PC,
mobile)

What operating system are you using?
```

```
What is the version number of the software?

Is there anything else we should know?
```

Shortly after the Alpha is released, issue reports start trickling in. The subject lines aren't exactly helpful, so Mowbray makes a note that he should include some advice on choosing good subject lines in the 'How to report a bug' sticky on the company forums. But, the bugs are a good indicator of where the main problems lie. The majority of the issues lie in two areas—the netbook conversion hasn't went very well, and there are lots of issues with online play:

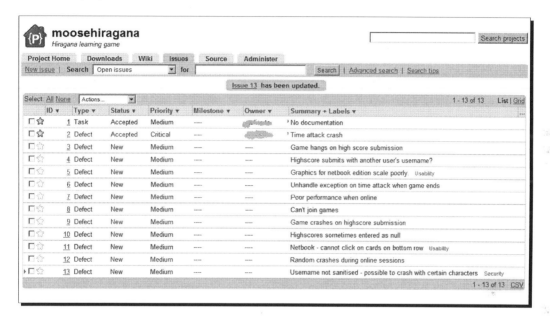

Quinn and Mowbray can now read through the bug reports, prioritizing them, and assigning them to the correct person. There are several duplicate reports. These can be closed (by setting their status to Duplicate) or filtered as appropriate.

Quinn decides to assign himself issue number 8—**Can't join games**. The bug report indicates that the user cannot see games even if they know for sure that there is a game available for them to join. He runs a few tests, and spots an issue with game listings which might cause games that have a name that begins with a non alphanumeric character to not appear in the listing. "That must be it!" he thinks to himself. "The user's friend must have made a game called '~~~Join me!!', hoping it would appear at the top of the list."

Quinn submits the patch and suggests that the bug has been fixed. The user comes back with a comment saying that the issue has **NOT** been fixed. They still can't see games.

At this point, Quinn is stumped. He's tested it in the office several times and it works fine. He asks one of the testers to try from home, and they report the same problem. So, what's the difference? Why does it work over the local network, but not online?

He examines the network code more closely, and notices that the timeout has been set to a ridiculously small value. Over the LAN, it's fine, but when you add internet connection lag into the mix, the connection is failing silently, and the user has no idea what's happening.

He fixes the problem, and the user reports that they're happy—they can now see games! Of course, the games are crashing, but that's another bug. One down, lots more to go!

While Quinn has been working on the network code, Mowbray has not been twiddling his thumbs. Using Google Code's filters, he was easily able to look at the issues with the Netbook build, and has created a new branch for re-designed art for the Netbook version. Now Netbook owning users are a lot happier because the interface works better for them, and they have specially designed the art that looks much nicer on their small screens.

So, what could have been a PR disaster—with the forums being flooded, and the team's inbox being filled up with angry mails—has been turned into a much more positive experience. Inevitably, there will be many angry users, but those who understand that this is an alpha test, and who want to do their bit, have been given the tools to do so. The team gets clear, concise bug reports which are easily filtered so that each member of the team can find the bugs that fall within their remit. Because of this the users will be happy too—they'll see more bugs fixed, more quickly, and better releases coming out, even sooner!

Why integrate with bug trackers?

Using a bug tracker has a lot of advantages. It makes it easy to keep track of outstanding issues, and see what issues have been fixed. It also makes it easy for your team members to see which issues are relevant to them. However, it's no good having a bug tracker if your team members forget to update it.

In most cases, when you commit a change it will be in response to an issue or bug filed against your project. You could commit your change, mention the bug in the commit messages, and then log on to the issue tracker's web interface and manually alter the status of the bug in there. That, however, is a lot of unnecessary repetition, especially when you think about the number of issues that you and your team will work with over the lifespan of your project.

It would be much more efficient to be able to associate bugs with commits automatically. The good news is that it's possible to do that for most of the popular bug trackers.

Integration with Google Code

Google Code is Google's free project hosting service for open source projects. It offers membership controls, Subversion and Mercurial repositories, an issue tracker, a wiki service, and a downloads section.

If your project is being released under an open source license, then Google Code is a great choice for your issue tracking hosting service.

Each project hosted on Google Code has its own page, which looks similar to the one shown in the following screenshot.

You can find the Subversion URL for your project by clicking the **Source** tab.

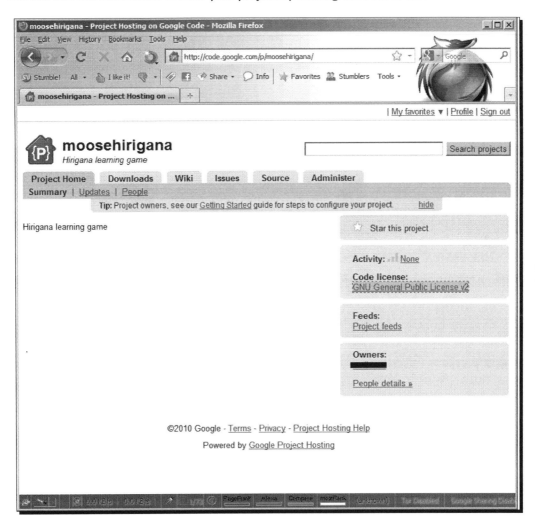

Time for action – using TortoiseSVN with Google Code

To achieve integration between TortoiseSVN and Google Code, you need to use a tool called **Gurtle**, which can be obtained from `http://code.google.com/p/gurtle`.

You will also need the Microsoft .NET Framework 2.0, which can be downloaded for free from: `http://www.microsoft.com/downloads/details.aspx?FamilyID=0856EACB-4362-4B0D-8EDD-AAB15C5E04F5`.

1. Download and install Gurtle. The installer is quite simple, just read and accept the terms and conditions, and then hit **Next** when prompted.

2. Next, bring up the TortoiseSVN Settings menu and go to **Hook Scripts | Issue Tracker Integration**.

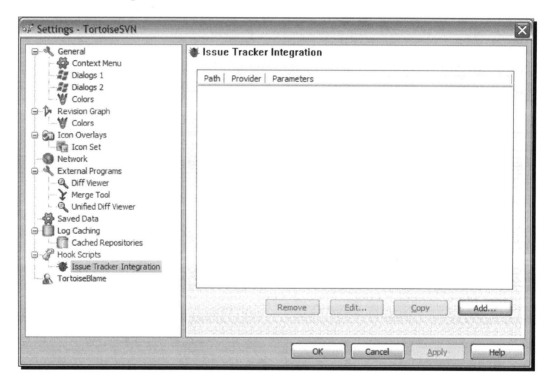

3. Click **Add...**.

4. On the screen that appears, enter the path to your working copy, and then click **Options**.

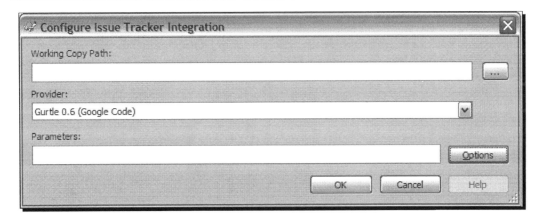

5. Enter the name of your project on Google Code in the box titled **Google Code Project Name** on the next screen, and click **Test**.

6. If you have entered the correct name, then you will see a message saying that the **Google Code Project appears valid and reachable**. Click **OK**.

7. Once you have the correct path, click **OK** to close the **Options** screen.

8. Next, you need to set the bugtraq properties. Right-click on the working copy folder and select **TortoiseSVN | Properties**.

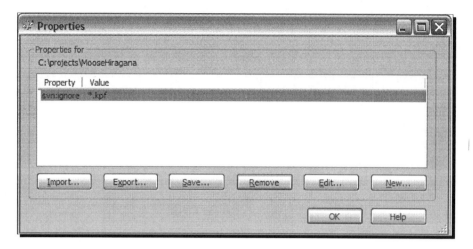

9. Click **New**.

10. Select **bugtraq:provideruuid** from the dropdown list, and enter the uuid of the Gurtle provider in the **Property value** box.

For a 32bit OS, the uuid is: **{91974081-2DC7-4FB1-B3BE-0DE1C8D6CE4E}**

For a 64bit OS, the uuid is: **{A0557FA7-7C95-485b-8F40-31303F762C57}**

11. Set **bugtraq:providerparams** to "`project=moosehiragana`".

What just happened?

You have just used a plugin called Gurtle to make Google Code work better with TortoiseSVN. You can get more information about customizing and using Gurtle at `http://code.google.com/p/gurtle/w/list`.

You can also learn more about using the Subversion features of Google Code at: `http://code.google.com/p/support/wiki/SubversionFAQ`

Pop quiz – Gurtle and Google Code

1. Gurtle is:

    a. Google's Turtle – a Google version of TortoiseSVN.

    b. A plugin for TortoiseSVN that adds extra features for working with Google Code.

    c. The name of the Subversion server used by Google Code.

Integration with Trac

Trac is a popular open source wiki and issue tracking system for software projects. Trac is released under a modified version of the BSD license. Its aim is to *help developers write great software, while staying out of the way.*

Trac is easy to set up, and there are many companies offering free Trac hosting too. You can find out more about Trac at: `http://trac.edgewall.org/`

Time for action – integration with Trac

TracExplorer is a suite of tools which includes integration plugins for Visual Studio and TortoiseSVN.

1. Download TracExplorer from `http://sourceforge.net/projects/vstrac/` — be sure to get the correct version (x86 or x64) for your operating system.

2. Open **TortoiseSVN | Settings**, go to **Hook Scripts | Configure Issue Tracker Integration**.

3. Set your **Working Copy Path**, and select **TracExplorer.TSVNTrac.TracProvider** from the **Provider** drop-down list.

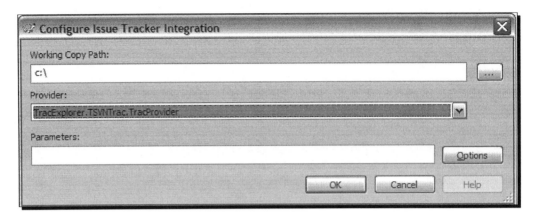

4. Click **Options**.

5. Click the **Add New Trac Server** icon, and add your Trac Server to Trac Explorer.

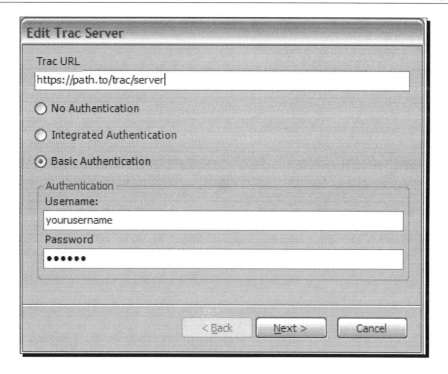

6. Next, select an issue from the list in **TracExplorer**.

7. Choose the statuses you want to use.

8. Now you should see a **Choose Tickets** button in TortoiseSVN, which presents you with a list of issues from your Trac Server.

What just happened?

You have set up TracExplorer so that you can see a list of Trac issues from within TortoiseSVN, and easily mark commits as being related to specific issues.

Integration with Redmine

Redmine is a flexible software project management system created using Ruby On Rails. You can learn more about Redmine at `http://www.redmine.org/`.

You can integrate Redmine with TortoiseSVN by using the TortoiseRedmine Plugin.

This plugin can be downloaded from `http://code.google.com/p/redmine-projects/downloads/list`

There are some detailed instructions for setting up the TortoiseRedmine plugin available on the project page at: `http://code.google.com/p/redmine-projects/wiki/InstallAndSetup`. Rather than duplicate the instructions (which may change for future versions) here, I recommend you refer to that page if you need assistance working with the plugin.

Integratation with Jira

Jira is a flexible issue tracking system that has some basic compatibility with Subversion out-of-the box. You can augment this with the help of the JiraSVN plugin, which can be downloaded from `http://csharptest-net.googlecode.com/files/SvnPluginInstall.msi`.

Users of the 64bit version of TortoiseSVN should download the version of the plugin found at: `http://code.google.com/p/csharptest-net/downloads/detail?name=SvnPluginInstall-x64.msi`.

The author of the plugin maintains an interesting blog about C# development and related issues, at `http://csharptest.net/`.

Installing the plugin is quite simple, simply a matter of running the `.msi` file and clicking **Next** when prompted.

Time for action – Jira and TortoiseSVN integration

1. Register the Jira plugin by going to **TortoiseSVN | Settings**, and selecting **Hook Scripts | Configure Issue Tracker Integration**, then clicking **Add**.

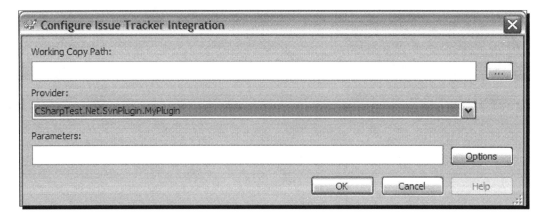

2. Select **CSharpTest.Net.SvnPlugin.MyPlugin** from the **Provider** dropdown, and enter the base path you want to use for check-ins in the **Working Copy Path**. In most cases, `c:\` is acceptable, or you could use your working copy directory if you wish.

3. Next, you need to set the bugtraq properties. Right-click on the working copy folder and select **TortoiseSVN | Properties**.

4. Click **New**.

5. Select **bugtraq:append** from the dropdown, and set the property value to **false**.

6. Repeat the process to set the following properties (changing the Jira URL if appropriate):
```
bugtraq:label = Defect {PREFIX}-
bugtraq:logregex = {Regular express match of defect ids}
bugtraq:message = {PREFIX}-%BUGID%
bugtraq:number = true
bugtraq:url = http://jira:8080/browse/{PREFIX}-%BUGID%
```

7. Create a new property called `jira:url` and set the value to your Jira URL.

8. You should now be able to perform a check-in and view issues using the **Jira Issues** button.

What just happened?

You have just set up the JiraSVN plugin to enable you to see, work with, and leave comments on Jira Issues in TortoiseSVN. This plugin enables you to see a list of issues without having to rely on using the web interface.

Working with other issue trackers

TortoiseSVN supports many other issue trackers, including Mantis, Microsoft Team Foundation Server, Artifacts, and Bugnet. There are too many bug trackers available for a complete list to be written here. If you use a bug tracker that has not been mentioned in this chapter, then it is worth checking to see if there is an existing plugin.

If there is not a plugin, then it may be possible to write one, or to take advantage of your bug tracker's pre-commit hook script to get some basic integration.

To take advantage of the pre-commit hook, you must define some properties on your project's folders. Some of those properties were listed earlier in this chapter. These properties should be set on folders for them to work. If you have different settings on a folder and a sub-folder, then the setting on the subfolder over-rides the parent folder's setting.

The `bugtraq:logregex` and `bugtraq:url` properties are useful even if you don't want to use any integration features. You can use those properties to, for example, turn all mentions of issues in log messages into links.

Properties for hook scripts

You can set TortoiseSVN to request the issue number that a bug relates to in a separate field, or you can use regular expressions to find the bug number from within the log message. If you set both options, any issue numbers found in the log message will over-ride those found in the issue number field.

The properties are:

- **bugtraq:append**: This property is true by default, meaning that the BugID is appended to the end of the log message. If set to false, then the BugID is inserted at the beginning of the log message.

- **bugtraq:label**: This defines the label shown next to the input box where the issue number is requested.

- **bugtraq:message**: This is used to define the message added to the end of the log message. It must contain `%BUGID%`—an example property value for this would be `Fixes: %BUGID%`

- **bugtraq:number**: This property is set to true by default, so that only numbers are permitted in the issue field. If your bug tracking system uses letters as well as numbers, then set this to false.

- **bugtraq:url**: This property should be set to the URL of your bug tracking system. The URL can be relative, or absolute. TortoiseSVN will use this URL to provide a link to the issue associated with the commit.

- **bugtraq:warnifnoissue**: This property is set to false by default. If it is set to true, then TortoiseSVN will warn the user if they attempt to make a commit without entering an issue number.

- **bugtraq:logregex**: If this property is set, TortoiseSVN will parse the log message to look for an issue number, allowing users to enter a messages in a human-readable format, such as "Fixes Bug: #45, #47 and #48". You can set your regular expression to look for any instances of a bug reference number. If you use this method, you will need to agree on consistent formatting for bug numbers within your team—if some people write Bug #123 while others write Bug No: 123, and others something different again, you'd need some fancy expressions to reliably catch everything! A simple regular expression to parse the "Fixes Bug:..." text shown previously is displayed in the following screenshot. The regular expression is quite simplistic. It could be improved to make it more likely to match even poorly written strings, for example, by using `[Bb]ugs` to catch "Fixes bugs:" as well as the intended "Fixes Bugs":

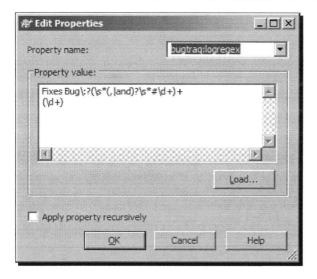

The previously shown regular expression has the following result in the log window.
Notice that the bug numbers have been converted to links:

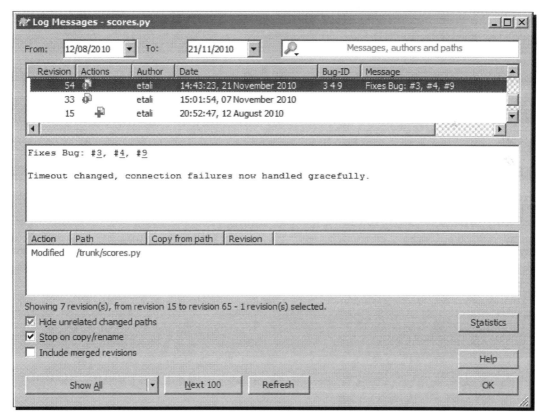

Even if you don't need to parse the log messages to get TortoiseSVN to work with your issue tracker, you can use the regular expressions parser to turn your log messages into links, making it easier to check out the issues at a later date.

Have a go hero – regular expressions

Even if your issue tracking system doesn't require the use of pre-commit hooks, it's worth playing with them to see what you can get them to do.

Using regular expressions to parse the commit log has several benefits, try writing a regular expression to parse your log message, and notice how much easier it is to pick out the issue numbers now!

If you aren't familiar with regular expressions, you can find a good regular expression tutorial at `http://www.regular-expressions.info/`.

Pop quiz – regular expressions

1. A regular expression is:

   a. A well formed piece of program code—for example, an IF statement.

   b. A connection string used to tell TortoiseSVN what Subversion server to connect to.

   c. An expression used to parse text and look for a piece that matches a specific pattern.

2. If both the regular expressions and the number property are used, then:

   a. `bugtraq:logregex` **overrides** `bugtraq:number`.

   b. `bugtraq:number` **overrides** `bugtraq:logregex`.

   c. It is not possible to set both, so this cannot happen.

Summary

This chapter looked at how to use TortoiseSVN with popular bug tracking systems. There are lots of different bug trackers, but TortoiseSVN is incredibly flexible and can be used with almost any system. Integrating TortoiseSVN with a bug tracking system makes it easy to associate patches with specific bugs, saving you time and effort, and ensuring that you always know what is going on in your project.

In this chapter you learned:

- Why it is important to work with issue trackers.
- How to integrate TortoiseSVN with the most popular issue trackers, including Google Code, Jira, Trac, and Redmine.
- How you might integrate TortoiseSVN with other issue trackers.

The next chapter will explain the issue of security, and how you can use SSH with TortoiseSVN to encrypt transmissions to and from your Subversion server.

10
Using SSL with TortoiseSVN

So far, we have focused on using TortoiseSVN itself. Our example Subversion server has been a rather simple, and in some ways insecure, one. If security is a priority – and it should be, if you are using Subversion in a business environment – then this chapter is for you.

In this chapter we shall:

- ◆ Learn about SSH and SSL
- ◆ Learn how to set up an Apache and Subversion setup on Linux
- ◆ Learn about public and private key pairs
- ◆ Learn how to use SSH with TortoiseSVN

So let's get started...

What are SSH and SSL?

You probably already have some awareness of SSH and SSL as forms of security. The terms SSH and SSL are thrown around quite frequently online by service providers and online shops trying to reassure their customers that their sites are safe to use.

SSL and SSH are often confused. **SSL** stands for **Secure Sockets Layer**. It typically uses port **443** for connections, and is most commonly used for transmitting financial information – for example for online banking, and online shopping.

SSH stands for **Secure Shell**. It usually uses port **22** for connections, and it is typically used for remote login and data transmission. Both SSH and SSL are incredibly secure. It is not practical for a normal hacker or 'script kiddie' to break the encryption which is used. This means that even if an attacker were able to eavesdrop on an SSH or SSL session, they would not be able to understand what is being transmitted.

SSH and SSL can be used to make your Subversion server more secure. Security may not be a concern for a small office with an internal-only server, but if your server is accessible via the Internet then it is a must.

Installing VisualSVN Server for Windows

VisualSVN Server is an easy-to-use SVN server for Windows. It works well out-of-the-box, is secure, and has a powerful but intuitive management console.

There are two versions of VisualSVN Server. The Standard Edition is a free download, and may be used for commercial purposes. The Enterprise Edition is not free ($950, at the time of writing), but adds extra features including remote administration and integrated Windows Authentication.

VisualSVN Server is by far the easiest way to set up a secure SVN server on Windows.

You can download VisualSVN Server from: `http://www.visualsvn.com/server/`.

Time for action – setting up VisualSVN Server

1. Download VisualSVN Server. The Standard Edition should suit the needs of most development teams.

2. Click **Next** to pass the first screen of the installer. Read the **License Agreement**, and, assuming you accept it, tick the checkbox to indicate such, and click **Next** again.

3. When prompted, select **VisualSVN Sever** and **Management Console**:

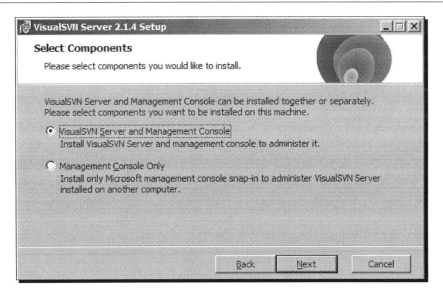

4. On the next screen, choose the directory you would like VisualSVN Server to be installed to, set the repository path, and the server port. The default server port should be acceptable for most people. Leave **use secure connection (https://)** ticked. If you want the server to be accessible over the internet, you may need to open the port on your router and/or firewall.

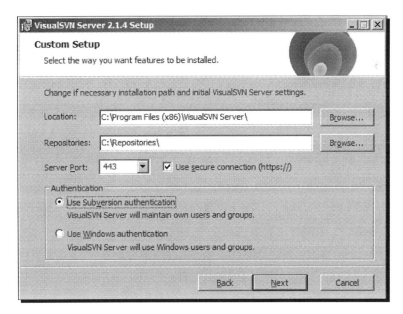

5. Click **Install**, and then when the installer completes, click **Finish**.

VisualSVN Server will launch. You should see a screen similar to the following screenshot:

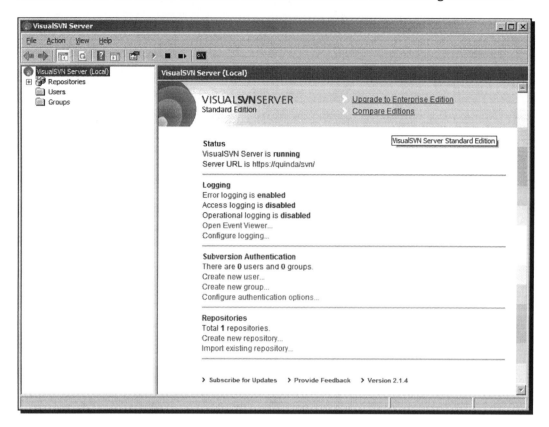

What just happened?

You have just installed the VisualSVN Server. This package includes Apache and Subversion, so you now have a working, secure Subversion setup.

The VisualSVN Server uses SSL security. It's easy to set up from an administrator's point of view, and even easier to use from a user's point of view. Your users can connect to the server without needing to do any complicated pre-setup.

Using VisualSVN Server

Now let's take a quick tour of the VisualSVN Server administration interface. The first thing you should notice is the tree structure down the left-hand side of the VisualSVN Server window. Under **Repositories**, you should see your existing repository. You can create a new repository by right-clicking on `Repositories`, and selecting **Create New Repository...**.

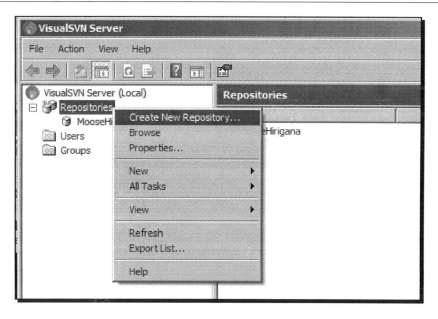

You can add users by right-clicking on **Users** and selecting **Create New User**:

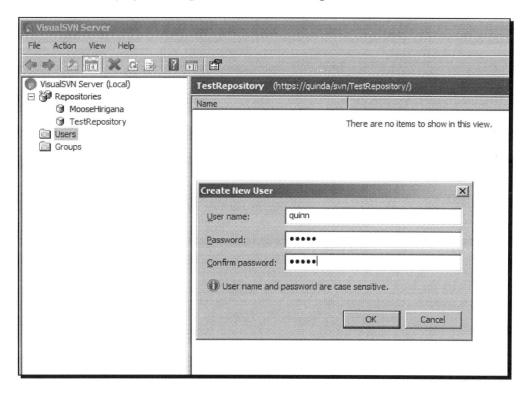

Groups can be created in a similar fashion.

To add users to a repository and set their permissions. Right-click on the repository in question and select **Properties**. This will bring up the **Properties** dialog:

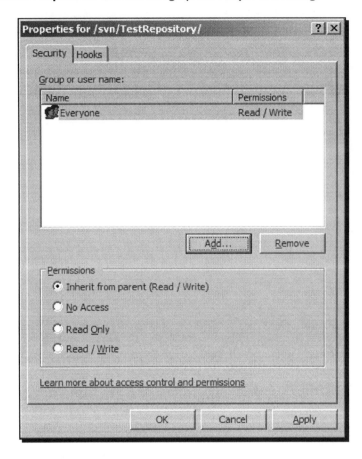

Click **Add**, and select the user (or group) you wish to add from the **Choose User or Group** dialog that appears:

Finally, click on each user, assign the correct permissions to them, and click **Apply**. In this case, we're limiting **Everyone** to **Read Only** access, except for Quinn, who is given **Read/Write** access:

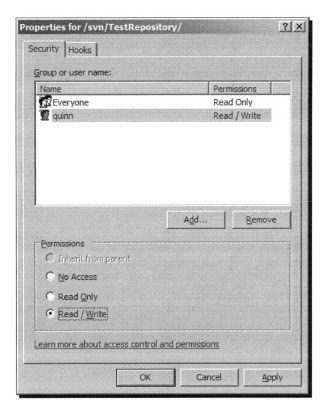

Pop quiz – all about SSH

1. SSH stands for:

   a. Secure Shell

   b. Special Secret Holder

   c. Secret Secure Holder

2. SSL Stands for:

   a. Secure Sockets Layer

   b. Secure Secrets Layer

   c. Secure Secret Locker

3. You can connect to Subversion via SSH using:

   a. `SSH+svn://`

   b. `File://`

   c. `Svn+ssh://`

   d. `http://`

Working with OpenSSH certificates

As a TortoiseSVN user, you may need to connect to a server that uses SSH. To do this, you will need to use a **keyfile**. The following instructions describe how to create public key and private key pairs on Linux. SSH key pairs can also be created on Windows by using **Puttygen** (`http://www.chiark.greenend.org.uk/~sgtatham/putty/download.html`).

Creating your public and private key pairs

To use **ssh-keygen**, you will need to be logged into the server as either the root user, or your SVN user.

Time for action – creating public and private key pairs

1. While logged in as the correct user, execute the following command:

```
ssh-keygen -b 1024 -t dsa -N YOURPASSPRHASEHERE -f mykeyfile
```

2. You should see something similar to the following (the key/fingerprint in this example are just made up examples):

```
ssh-keygen -b 1024 -t dsa -N whatevermykeyis -f mykeyfile
Generating public/private dsa key pair.
Your identification has been saved in keyfile.
Your public key has been saved in keyfile.pub.
The key fingerprint is:
1a:a9:11:1d:2b:c2:e5:5a:65:29:df:8a:1d:4c:69:3c root@debian
The key's randomart image is:
+--[ DSA 1024]----+
|                 |
|                 |
|          . .    |
|         . * o   |
|        + E o    |
|        + @ B    |
|       . o * .   |
|        o o o    |
|         . . o   |
+-----------------+
```

3. If you want to make keys for more than one user, run the command again, specifying a different name instead of `mykeyfile`.

4. For each keyfile, you should see two files: one called `mykeyfile`, which is the private key, and another called `mykeyfile.pub`, which is the public key. Copy the private key to your Windows desktop.

5. Download **PuTTYgen** from `http://www.chiark.greenend.org.uk/`
`~sgtatham/putty/download.html`Run PuTTYgen and go to **Conversions |
Import**, then select your key.

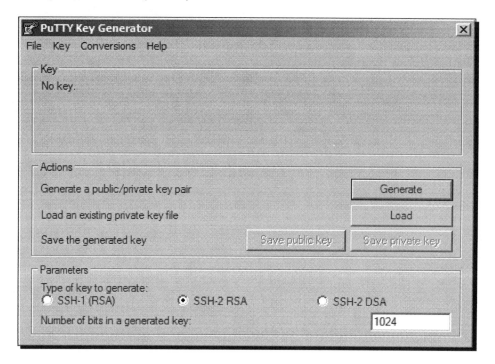

6. Enter your passphrase when prompted.

7. Click **Save public key**.

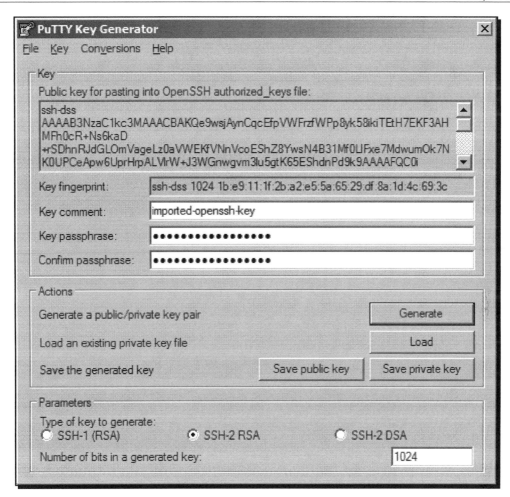

8. Save the key using an appropriate file name, with a `.ppk` extension.

9. To test the key, use PuTTY (available for free from `http://www.chiark.greenend.org.uk/~sgtatham/putty/`) to connect to your SVN server – fill in the hostname box, and add your `.ppk` file under **SSH | Auth**:

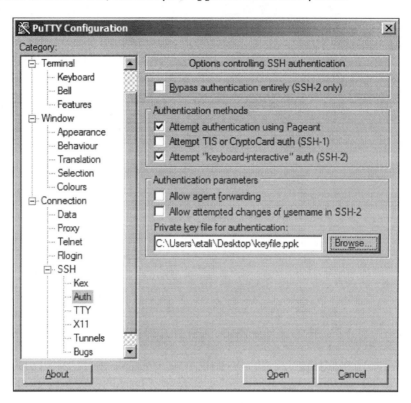

10. Save the session, and attempt a connection. You should see something similar to the following:

```
login as: svn
Authenticating with public key "imported-openssh-key"
( success ( 1 2 ( ANONYMOUS EXTERNAL ) ( edit-pipeline
svndiff1 absent-entries ) ) )
```

What just happened?

You have just created your public and private keys, and converted the public key into a format which can be used on Windows. Make a note of the name that you used in PuTTY, as this will be used by TortoiseSVN later to connect to the server.

Public Key and **Private Key** cryptography is popular in computing. It is used by a number of standards – not just SSH, but **Transport Layer Security** (**TLS**, the successor of SSL), and PGP too.

Public key cryptography is different to other methods because it is **asymmetric**. This means that the key that encrypts the message is not the one that decrypts it. Users of public key cryptographic methods have a pair of keys – one is a public key, the other is a private key.

As the name suggests, the public key can be shared freely. Messages are encrypted using a user's public key, and can only be decrypted with the private key. So, users can share their public key with anyone they expect to communicate with, while keeping their private key secret and secure.

Hybrid systems

The SSL and TLS family of encryption schemes are actually hybrid algorithms. They use a key exchange algorithm and transmit data using that key and a symmetric key algorithm.

There is, of course, some concern – how do you know if the public key really does belong to the person you think it does? This can be ensured via the use of certificate authorities which issue digital certificates that contain information about the owner of each certificate.

Pop quiz – public keys and private keys

1. With Public and Private Key Systems you:

    a. Encrypt data with your private key and decrypt it with your public key.

    b. Encrypt data with your public key, and decrypt it with your private key.

    c. Use the public key to sign your message to make sure it hasn't been tampered with.

2. Asymmetric encryption systems are:

    a. More secure than symmetric systems.

    b. Less secure than symmetric systems.

    c. Just as secure as symmetric systems, but less processor intensive.

Using Pageant to store connection details

If you find using PuTTY to store your connection details to be a cumbersome process, then you might prefer to use Pageant, which can be downloaded from:

`http://www.chiark.greenend.org.uk/~sgtatham/putty/download.html`.

Pageant allows you to store keys for multiple servers, and is useful if you need to manage a lot of keys. Pageant runs in the taskbar, and has a simple interface, simply click **Add Key**, and browse to the location of your Private Key:

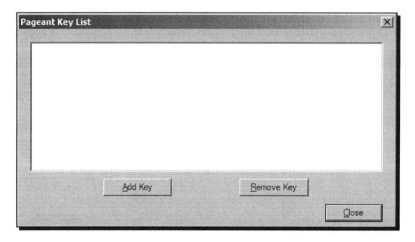

Pop quiz – connecting to Subversion with SSH

1. Pageant can be used to:
   a. Store your public keys
   b. Store your private keys
   c. Store connection details for SSH servers
   d. All of the above
2. The key phrases we are using are:
   a. 1024 bit
   b. 256 bit
   c. 64 bit
   d. 512 bit

Using pre-commit hooks

Server-side hooks were discussed in an earlier chapter, but there are a few things that they cannot be used effectively for.

One such example is checking to see whether a file has been modified recently.

Quinn goes to a meeting with his lawyer, and discovers that the way he had been updating the copyright notice in files inside the MooseHiragana project was wrong. The copyright year should not be changed for every file at the start of a new year – it should only be updated if the content of the file has actually been changed that year. Modifying each file's copyright date manually would be an error-prone process. Fortunately, there's an easy way to make sure you never forget to update the copyright year, using a pre-commit hook:

Time for action – using a pre-commit hook in TortoiseSVN

Quinn decides to make use of a pre-commit script provided by the makers of TortoiseSVN. The script is available from TortoiseSVN's Google Code Project, which checks `.cpp` and `.h` files and shows an error for every file the user forgot to update the copyright year. It's a simple matter to change the `.cpp` to `.py` so that the Python files in the project are checked.

1. Download the script from: `http://code.google.com/p/tortoisesvn/ source/browse/trunk/contrib/hook-scripts/client-side/checkyear. js`. If necessary, modify it to suit the file type, and copyright message format, of your project.

2. Make a note of where you save the file; you'll need the path later.

3. Bring up the TortoiseSVN right-click menu and select **Settings**.

4. In the **Settings** dialog box that appears, select **Hook Scripts**, then click **Add**.

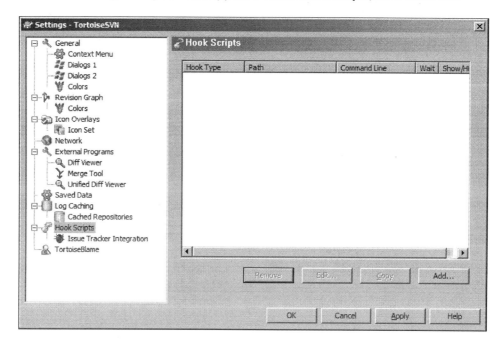

5. Set the **Hook Type** to **Pre-Commit Hook**. Tick **Wait for the script to finish**, point the working copy path to your working copy, and in the **Command Line To Execute** field enter **wscript c:\checkyear.js**– assuming you saved the file to your user folder. If you have saved the script somewhere other than your user folder, then enter **wscript /path/to/checkyear.js**.

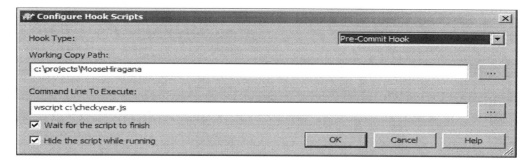

6. In the preceding screenshot, **Hide the script while running** is ticked. That is probably how you will want to have the hook script set up in the long term (Command boxes are pretty ugly, and can confuse non-technical users), but for testing purposes it can be useful to leave this unchecked, so that you can see what is happening.

Now, when you make a commit, your files will be checked, and you will be alerted if you are trying to commit a file that does not have an up-to-date copyright year:

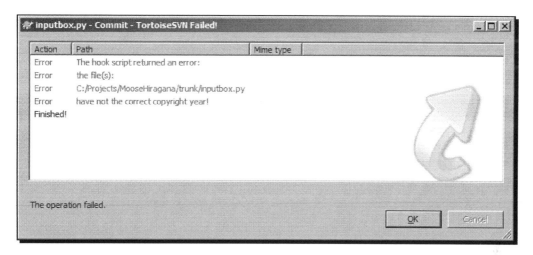

What just happened?

You have just set up a client-side pre-commit hook that will check the contents of the files you are committing for an up-to-date copyright notice. If the copyright notice contains the wrong year, you will be informed.

You can use client-side pre-commit-hooks for many other purposes, for example, you could check to make sure that the build was successful, or that the code has been run through a test-suite successfully, before a commit is allowed.

Summary

This chapter looked at how to use TortoiseSVN with SSH and SSL, and how to set up client-side hook scripts. This is important if you want to ensure that your Subversion server is as secure as possible, and that connections cannot be eavesdropped upon.

In this chapter you learned:

◆ What SSH and SSL are and why are they important

◆ How to set up VisualSVN Server

◆ How to create public and private key pairs

◆ How to use the keys with TortoiseSVN

◆ How to use client-side pre-commit hooks

SSL security is easy to use once it's set up. It doesn't get in the way, and it adds an extra layer of security.

This chapter concludes the main part of the book. I hope you have found it useful in learning how to use TortoiseSVN. The appendix which follows this chapter explains some of the more important commands which you can use via the command line – you don't have to use the command line to interact with Subversion if you do not want to, but there are times when it is convenient to do so, and you may find its speed and flexibility useful.

Command-line Reference

TortoiseSVN allows you to access Subversion's commands from within windows, easily performing check-ins, setting properties, viewing the repository, and performing other tasks. However, there may be occasions when you will find it quicker and easier to do some actions via the command-line. You don't have to use the command-line if you don't want to, but it can be a powerful tool when used well.

This appendix contains:

- ◆ A list of the components of Subversion
- ◆ A list of the Subversion command-line commands
- ◆ A list of properties used by Subversion

Getting the command-line tools

The SVN command line client tools are shipped with VisualSVN, so if you have already installed VisualSVN Server (which was discussed in *Chapter 10, Using SSH With TortoiseSVN*), then you will have the command-line tools.

If you have not already installed VisualSVN Sever, then you can download the files from one of the sites listed at:

```
http://subversion.apache.org/packages.html#windows
```

The **CollabNet client** is a free download, although registration is required. If you do not want to provide registration information, then I recommend the **SlikSVN client**, although any of the clients listed on the `http://subversion.apache.org/` site will work.

Subversion's components

Subversion is made up of several components. Each one serves a different purpose:

- `svn`: The main command-line program
- `svnversion`: Reports the revision of the working copy
- `svnlook`: Used to inspect the repository
- `svndumpfilter`: Filters the repository stream
- `od_dav_svn`: The SVN Apache Module
- `svnserve`: The SVN Server
- `svnsync`: Used to mirror a repository

Protocols supported by Subversion

Subversion supports several protocols. They are:

- `file://`: Used to reference a path on the local machine
- `http://`: Used to reference a path on an Apache web server
- `https://`: Used to reference a path on an Apache web server using SSL
- `svn://`: Used to reference a path to an SVNServe server
- `svn+ssh://`: Used to reference an SVNServe server using SSH

Subversion command-line reference

The following table provides a list of SVN commands:

Getting help

Subversion has an extensive help system. To view the list of available commands, use SVN Help. Using `svn help <command>` will give detailed information on the usage of the specified command, along with any switches that can be used with that command.

Syntax	Usage
`svn help`	Shows a list of commands.
`svn help <command>`	Shows detailed help for that command.

Working with working copies

Syntax	Usage
svn checkout "/PATH/branch-name/"	Performs a checkout, creating a working copy of the branch (or trunk) specified.
svn checkout "/PATH/branch-name/" <foldername>	As above, but checks out into a folder with the name specified.
svn update -r<revision-number> "/PATH/TO/UPDATE_FROM"	Updates your working copy to the specified revision (or the latest revision, if no revision number is specified).
svn add	Used to add files to version control. Switches are filename, foldername (in which case subfolders and files will be added), * (all items will be added, recursively, ignoring already versioned folders), and * --force (which will recourse into versioned directories).
svn copy "source" "destination"	Copies from the source path to the destination path.
svn move "source "destination"	Moves files from the source path to the destination path.
svn delete "/PATH"	Deletes the target path.
svn revert "/path/to/file"	Reverts changes to the specified file or folder.
svn log "/PATH"	Shows log messages.
svn blame "/PATH"	Shows commits and messages for the given path.
svn diff "/PATH/filename"	See changes to filename.
svn diff "/PATH/file@1" "/PATH/file@3"	See changes to filename between revisions one and three.
svn merge "URL1" "URL2" "/PATH/filename"	Apply the diff of URL1 and URL2 to filename.
svn commit "/PATH"	Commit changes to a file or folder
svn resolve "/PATH"	Resolve a conflict.
svn cleanup "/PATH"	Remove locks and complete operations – acts recursively.
svn lock "/PATH"	Get a lock on the given path.
svn unlock "/PATH"	Releases a lock on a given path.
svn cat "/PATH/filename"	Prints the contents of the file to the screen.
svn status "/PATH"	Shows the status of the path.
svn propdel <PROPERTY> "/PATH"	Deletes <PROPERTY>.

Syntax	Usage
svn propget <PROPERTY> "/PATH"	Gets the value of <PROPERTY>
svn proplist "/PATH"	Lists the properties of /PATH
svn propset <PROPERTY> <VALUE> "/PATH"	Sets <PROPERTY> to <VALUE> for /PATH

Arguments for commands

These arguments can be added to SVN commands to modify the default behavior. For example, **svn update** will update to the latest revision by default, but svn update -r101 will update to revision 101.

Argument	Usage
-m "Message content"	Adds a message
-q	Quiet
-v	Verbose
-r<number>	Revision number
-c	Change
-t	Transaction
-R	Recursive
-N	Non recursive

Properties and statuses

The following are the possible statuses that an item can have. If there is no status listed beside an item, that means there have been no modifications.

Property	Meaning
A	Added
D	Deleted
M	Modified
R	Replaced
C	Conflict
X	External
I	Ignored
?	Not found in repository
!	Missing
~	Type changed

B
Pop Quiz Answers

The answers to the pop quizzes from each chapter are provided here for your reference. How did you score?

Chapter 1: Setting up TortoiseSVN

Pop quiz - subversion concepts

1	2	3
b	c (In the context of Subversion)	b

Chapter 2: Getting Started with TortoiseSVN

Pop quiz - working with TortoiseSVN

1	2	3
c	b	b

Chapter 3: Creating and Applying Patches

Pop quiz - working with TortoiseSVN

1	2	3
a	a	a

Chapter 4: Status Information and Conflict Management

Pop quiz - working with TortoiseSVN

1	2	3
c	c	c

Chapter 5: Branching and Merging

Pop quiz - working with TortoiseSVN

1	2	3	4	5
c	c	c	a	d

Chapter 6: Working with Revision Logs

Pop quiz 1 - revision graphs

1	2
c	b

Pop quiz 2 – working with your view

1	2	3
d	a	c

Chapter 7: Exporting and relocating Working Copies

Pop quiz - working with your working copy

1	2	3
c	d	a

Chapter 8: Keyword Substitution with SubWCRev

Pop quiz 1 - getting to grips with SubWCRev

1	2
b	a

Pop quiz 2 - keyword substitution switches

1	2	3
a	b	c

Chapter 9: Using TortoiseSVN with Bug Tracking Systems

Pop quiz 1 - Gurtle and Google Code

1
b

Pop quiz 2 - regular expressions

1	2
c	a

Chapter 10: Using SSH with TortoiseSVN

Pop quiz 1 - all about SSH

1	2	3
a	a	c

Pop quiz 2 - public keys and private keys

1	2
a	a

Index

Thank you for buying
TortoiseSVN 1.7 Beginner's Guide

About Packt Publishing

Packt, pronounced 'packed', published its first book "*Mastering phpMyAdmin for Effective MySQL Management*" in April 2004 and subsequently continued to specialize in publishing highly focused books on specific technologies and solutions.

Our books and publications share the experiences of your fellow IT professionals in adapting and customizing today's systems, applications, and frameworks. Our solution based books give you the knowledge and power to customize the software and technologies you're using to get the job done. Packt books are more specific and less general than the IT books you have seen in the past. Our unique business model allows us to bring you more focused information, giving you more of what you need to know, and less of what you don't.

Packt is a modern, yet unique publishing company, which focuses on producing quality, cutting-edge books for communities of developers, administrators, and newbies alike. For more information, please visit our website: www.packtpub.com.

About Packt Open Source

In 2010, Packt launched two new brands, Packt Open Source and Packt Enterprise, in order to continue its focus on specialization. This book is part of the Packt Open Source brand, home to books published on software built around Open Source licences, and offering information to anybody from advanced developers to budding web designers. The Open Source brand also runs Packt's Open Source Royalty Scheme, by which Packt gives a royalty to each Open Source project about whose software a book is sold.

Writing for Packt

We welcome all inquiries from people who are interested in authoring. Book proposals should be sent to author@packtpub.com. If your book idea is still at an early stage and you would like to discuss it first before writing a formal book proposal, contact us; one of our commissioning editors will get in touch with you.

We're not just looking for published authors; if you have strong technical skills but no writing experience, our experienced editors can help you develop a writing career, or simply get some additional reward for your expertise.

Managing Software Development with Trac and Subversion

ISBN: 978-1-847191-66-3   Paperback: 120 pages

Simple project management for software development.

1. Managing software development projects simply

2. Configuring a project management server

3. Installing, configuring, and using Trac

Project Management with dotProject: Implement, Configure, Customize, and Maintain your DotProject Installation

ISBN: 978-1-847191-64-9   Paperback: 232 pages

A complete beginner's guide to every aspect of setting up and administering your dotProject installation

1. Install and use the dotProject project management system

2. Customize and extend dotProject

3. Work with reports and Gantt charts

Please check **www.PacktPub.com** for information on our titles